RISC Microprocessors,

History and Overview

Patrick H. Stakem

© 2013

3rd edition, 3rd in Computer Architecture Series

Table of Contents

Photo credits:
Photos are from the author's collection, or courtesy, John Culver, cpushack.com

Introduction

It is hard to generalize about the RISC approach, because for every principle discussed, a counter-example in implementation can be found. However, in RISC, most instructions execute in one cycle. RISC machines tend to have a small instruction set, and complex instructions are built up from primitive ones. This follows the observation that, generally, the simple instructions are the most frequently used and the more complex instructions less so. The use of the RISC technique began around 1990, and has now become mainstream. It evolved out of a time when memory was an expensive asset, and memory utilization was an issue.

Decoding instructions and addressing modes are a major bottleneck to speed, so simplified instruction encoding and few data addressing modes are preferable.

Single cycle execution improves interrupt latency and response determinism. A load/store architecture will have many on-chip registers to hold data currently in use. A RISC CPU is tightly coupled to memory, and achieves a high data bandwidth with a sophisticated cache. Instruction execution is pipelined. Instruction decoding is streamlined because there are fewer instructions, and they are relatively simple, with perhaps a single address mode. In a RISC machine, microcode is to be avoided, and yet some RISC architectures use it.

Here's a top level approach to a RISC implementation. Eliminate all instructions that can't execute in 1 clock cycle. Move complexity from hardware to software. Add more hardware, as feasible, to include more complex instructions. There are no "subroutines" or loops at the machine language level allowed. Don't slow down the majority of instructions for the minority.

4

The 90/10 rule says that about 90% of real code are simple instructions, such as load/store, alu ops, etc. Not much can be done to speed up the remaining 10% of complex instructions.

The instructions/task metric is low for cisc; high for risc; i.e., risc uses more instructions to get the job done, but they are faster instructions. Non-RISC instructions get more done, per instruction. For example, the string compare instruction in the IA-32 architecture is actually a loop in microcode.

Author

The author received his BSEE from Carnegie Mellon University, and Masters in Computer Science and Applied Physics from the Johns Hopkins University. He has always worked in the aerospace sector, supporting NASA projects at all of the NASA Centers. He has taught for the graduate Engineering Science and Computer Science Departments at Loyola University in Maryland, and currently teaches Embedded Systems for the Johns Hopkins University, Whiting School of Engineering, Engineering for Professionals Program. He developed and taught a course in RISC architecture for Loyola.

The Performance Equation

The amount of time to execute any particular piece of software can be expressed as:
$$T = N * C * 1/f$$
Where N = number of instructions, C = clock cycles per instruction, and f is the clock frequency for the processor. The term instruction here refers to the number of machine instructions. An expression in a higher level language can result in multiple machine instructions.

So, to minimize the time taken to do a software task, we can reduce N, reduce C, or increase f.

Increases in the clock frequency, and the frequency of operation of the hardware comes with advances in technology, and can be assumed. There are numerous architectural approaches to reduce C, and the goal of the RISC approach is to reduce this term to 1. Unfortunately, this usually means a corresponding increase in N, the number of instructions to accomplish a task.

If we have very simple instructions, we may need more of them to accomplish a task. Simple instructions are easy to streamline and speed up by a variety of techniques. Some tasks are very difficult to reduce to the point of taking one cycle; the multiply and divide for example. Some tasks inherently need time to complete, particularly those with loops. Consider the block move instructions in the IA-32 architecture (sometimes called a software DMA). Here we have one instruction, $N=1$, but it can take hundreds of cycles to complete ($C = 100$'s). Unless we have enough hardware to move hundreds of data items simultaneously, this is a problem. We can always throw more hardware at it. As technology rides the exponential complexity law, termed Moore's law, we have more hardware to work with. But we have to be clever about how this hardware is managed at run time.

Some RISC approaches to enhance speed of execution:

Load-Store Architecture

In a load-store architecture, memory is only accessed by a load instruction (read from memory), or a store instruction (write to memory). All of the operational instructions (math, logical, etc.) operate only on data in registers.

Superscalar

The superscalar approach to instruction execution involves parallelism. It allows for execution of more than a single instruction per clock cycle, by using additional hardware to implement additional function units such as the ALU or multiplier. Multiple instructions at a time are fetched and fed to separate execution pipelines. Additional hardware is required to check for data dependencies at runtime. In the case of a branch or change in the flow of control, the assumption of sequential execution is no longer met, and pipelines and other resources have to be reloaded. The superscalar approach dates from Cray's CDC 6600 machine in 1965. Superscalar was a natural fit for RISC architectures, and essentially all CPU's from about 1998 on are superscalar.

Since the superscalar approach involves multiple parallel functional units, a key feature is the instruction dispatcher, which decides where the next instruction to be executed goes. The goal is to keep all of the hardware busy, all of the time. The sustained execution rate, without changes in context, is more than 1 instruction per clock. The performance depends on the intrinsic parallelism in the instruction stream; some sequences of instructions cannot be optimized. This is referred to as instruction-level parallelism. Sometimes, this can be corrected at the compiler level by instruction re-ordering. Branches and other changes in the flow of control are a problem.

As the level of hardware parallelism increases from 2 to 4 to greater, the cost of checking dependencies increases. This is a cost in hardware complexity. The practical limit to the number of simultaneously executing instructions is bounded by the complexity of checking dependencies, and is around six instructions.

In the limit, a multicore processor is superscalar, but the processors are not executing from the same instruction stream, and the entire CPU architecture is replicated, not just functional units within a CPU.

Scoreboarding

Scoreboarding is a technique to manage multiple resources such as pipelines, registers, and ALU's, to support dynamic scheduling. It was first used on the circa-1964 CDC 6400 mainframe. The technique requires a series of data tables, that indicate the current use of resources. Resources can be idle, busy, or available. The hardware monitors the resources, and uses the next available resource for the current instruction.

Speculative execution

In speculative execution, the CPU may proceed simultaneously down both paths of a data dependent branch (taken and non-taken) until the result is known, at which point one path of execution can be discarded. This takes additional hardware and resources, but saves time. Speculative execution reduces the time-cost of conditional branches. Branch prediction can also be used, and a history of branch addresses can be kept.

Register Windows

This technique was developed to optimize the performance of procedure calls, and was implemented in the Berkeley SPARC architecture. It also found use in the AMD 29k and Intel i960.
Registers are a key resource, particularly in a load-store architecture. The allocation of registers dynamically at run time is the issue addressed by the concept of register windows. Registers are scoreboarded. In the Berkeley design, only 8 registers are visible to the running program, out of a total of 64 available. The 64 are called the register file, and a set of 8 are called a register window. They are allocated as windows, and only 8 items (windows of registers) are tracked, not 64 (registers). Registers windows are a type of stack data cache.

In the AMD 29k, the windows can be of variable size. The SPARC architecture increased the number of register windows as technology allowed.

SIMD

Single Instruction, Multiple Data (SIMD) refers to a class of parallel computers that perform the same operations on multiple data items simultaneously. This is data level parallelism, which is found in multimedia (video and audio) data used in gaming applications. The SIMD approach evolved from the vector supercomputers of the 1970's, which operated upon a vector of data with a single operation. Sun Microsystems introduced SIMD operations in their SPARC architecture in 1995. A popular application of SIMD architecture is Intel's MMX (Multimedia

Extensions) instruction set circa 1996 for the X-86 architecture.

VLIW

Very Long Instruction Word (VLIW) computer architectures take advantage of instruction-level parallelism. Within the long instruction word are instructions that can be executed simultaneously. These instructions are discovered by the compiler, and grouped together into the VLIW's. Thus, some of the inherent complexity of the problem is removed from the hardware, and placed on the software. The term and the concept of VLIW are attributed to computer architect Josh Fisher at Yale in the 1980's. The first microprocessor to use VLIW techniques was Intel's i860. Other RISC techniques include:

- Out-of-order execution is used as an approach to increase the work being done per clock cycle. Instructions are selected to be executed not necessarily in program order, but rather in the order that the associated data is available. This minimizes idle time in the CPU, and is an outgrowth of the dataflow approach in computer architecture. The first out-of-order risc microprocessor was the floating point unit of IBM's POWER-1, in 1990. It was also applied in the Intel PentiumPro, AMD K5, the PowerPC 601, SPARC64, Dec Alpha 21264, and MIPS R10000. The cost of out-of-order execution is increased complexity in the logic. The technique became mainstream around 1995.
  The out-of-order approach relies on being able to find operations that have their associated operands ready. It is complicated by read-after-write conflicts, branching, and interrupts. Sometimes, a pipeline stall is unavoidable. The logical ordering of the instructions has to be kept, to produce the correct results. Out of order processing has its best benefits when the pipeline is expanded. Register renaming is also used to support the out-of-order execution.

- Pipeline

Here, we break up instructions into sub steps, such as fetch opcode, decode, fetch operands, alu operations, and write result, with the idea of increasing throughput. In a pipeline architecture, more instructions are completed every clock time than in a simple architecture, where only one instruction is completed. This takes additional hardware, and complexity, to accomplish. Essentially parallel hardware allows for simultaneous sub-steps. More stages in the pipeline (the "superpipeline") requires a lot more hardware, but vastly increases throughput. The Pentium 4 implements a 20-stage pipeline. Ideally, a pipelined processor can complete an instruction every clock cycle. During the processing of an instruction, if the instruction has to wait for some item or results, the pipeline stalls as its steady-state flow is interrupted. This is called a bubble in the pipeline; essentially a pipeline NOP. Out-of-order execution of instructions can prevent bubbles from happening. Changes in the flow of control, due to a branch or interrupt can disrupt the smooth functioning of the pipeline, and cause the pipeline to be reloaded. Conditional branches, where the path is not determined until the instruction has executed, are a particular problem. Sometimes this is addressed by speculative execution, which uses additional hardware to simultaneously follow both paths of the branch, until the results are known, at which point one path is discarded. Branch prediction techniques are also applied. The downside of a pipelined processor is that it may be difficult to determine exact latency in the case of interrupts, which is needed in a hard real time environment.

Within the pipeline, operand fetch and store are also problematic, as they involve memory operations, which are slower that the CPU. RISC architectures tend to employ a load/store approach, where registers can be loaded rom or stored to memory, but arithmetic and logical operations only operate on data in registers, which share silicon with the CPU.

- Microcode

  RISC machines tend to avoid microcode, and instead use hard-wired instruction decode by combinatorial logic for speed. In a microcoded system, the instruction opcode is applied to a special read-only memory, and the steps in the execution are read from the memory. This approach has the advantage that the instruction set can be extended to add new instructions, by extending the microcode. But it is not faster than using simple logic and state machines, producing a "hardwired" instruction set. Complexity in the instruction set, such as complex addressing modes, complicate the instruction decode. Above the microcode level is the "programmer-visible" level. If microcode is used, the decoding rom is referred to as the control store, and its contents define how instructions are executed. It is possible to have more than one interpretation (ISA) if the hardware allows it. The microcode concept goes back to the 1947 IBM Whirlwind computer.

RISC chips

This section discusses the microprocessor chips that implemented the RISC philosophy. Now that RISC is mainstream, almost all current processors have RISC heritage.

AMD 29k

The circa 1985 AMD 29000 series addressed the embedded market, including telecomm, laser printers, and networking. It was a 32-bit machine, that went on to influence AMD's K5 and K6 chips, which implemented the Intel x86 ISA. The K5 translated x86 to 29k instructions on the fly.

The 29k was a Harvard design, superscalar with a 5-stage pipeline. It supported out-of-order and speculative execution. It was essentially designer Mike Johnson's thesis project. It had a large number of registers (192), and a small number of instructions (112). It included a memory management unit and a branch target cache for virtual addresses. It was a load/store machine with a single addressing mode. All instructions were 32 bits wide, with an op code and 3 operand fields. The 3 operand format reduced the instructions/task term of the performance equation.

Dec Alpha

The DEC Alpha chip was a 64-bit, superscalar, superpipelined architecture. It used the load/store architecture, and supported 32 integer and 32 floating point registers. R31 and F31 were defined as zero. The architecture was a derivative of the circa-1986 PRISM.

DEC 21064

DEC 21164

Addressing was 64-bit virtual, 34-bit physical, and little-endian. The chip used register scoreboarding and result bypassing for speed. There were no condition codes. 128-bit internal data paths were used. Other optimization techniques included in the design included read/write re-ordering, branch prediction, and out-of-order execution.

The instructions were all 32-bits long, with a 6-bit opcode. There were four classes of instruction: Palcode, conditional branch, load/store, and operate/floating.

The PALcode was an instruction set extension via a hardware abstraction layer. It resided in ROM, and supported VAX family instructions. Multiprocessor coherency was provided by cache snooping.

Before the full power of the Alpha chips could be unleashed, DEC was bought out by Compaq Computer. Production of the Alpha was shifted to Samsung. The Alpha Design Group became Alpha Processor, Inc which later became API Networks, Inc. Compaq dumped the Alpha design.

There were several models of the Alpha chip. The 21064 featured a 7-stage integer pipeline, and a 10-stage pipeline for floating point. It had 4 functional units, the integer, floating, branch, and load/store. It also had an integral MMU. The 21066 added integrated dram support. The 21164 was the last model. It operated at 366 through 800 MHz, and was fabricated by Samsung. An "A" version added video-related instructions, and a "B" version extended the clock to 1 GHz. The 21264 was to have out-of-order execution for up to 80 instructions, but by this time, the Design team had been disbanded. The 21364, on the drawing board, was targeted to scalable multiprocessor systems, and had onboard switching/routing for I/O.

ARM

ARM was the first commercial reduced instruction set computer (RISC) microprocessor, circa 1985. ARM processors represent a non-traditional RISC design, optimized for low power consumption. The chip's high power efficiency gave it an edge in battery powered portable equipment. ARM currently has one of the best MIPS per watt ratings in the industry.

The ARM RISC processor project was started by Acorn Computers of Cambridge, England, in 1983. The current ARM line started with a design effort by Advanced RISC Machine, Ltd. a company that licensed designs for fabrication.

The major applications for the device are in 32-bit embedded control, and the portable computing. ARM describes an architecture for a family of processors, 32-bits in word size (now extended to 64-bits). There are only 10 basic instruction types. On-chip is set of 16 registers, a barrel shifter, and hardware multiplier. The ARM was designed as a static device, meaning that the clock may be arbitrarily slowed or stopped, with no loss of internal state. This also affects power consumption. The ARM6 core had 37k transistors. The low-end member of the family, the ARM2 (86C010) implemented the core, with no cache or memory management unit (MMU). The ARM3 (86C020) included the core plus a 4-kilobyte unified cache, a coprocessor interface, and semaphore support for multiprocessing. The ARM600 (86C600) added an MMU (memory management unit) and a write buffer. Other members of the family included the 86C060, and the 26-bit bus 86C061 version, that provided compatibility with earlier products, and the ARM 610.

The ARM2 had a 32-bit data bus with a 26-bit address space. It implemented twenty-seven 32-bit registers. The program counter was 24 bits. The design was simple and streamlined; being implemented in 30,000 transistors, half the count of Motorola's contemporary 68000 chip.

Acorn had design experience with RISC designs going back to 1983, and marketed their RISC-based Archimedes computers in Europe by 1987. Originally a dynamic logic design for minimal silicon area, the complexities of this approach convinced the designers that the core should be fully static. An asynchronous ARM design still exists.

The ARM 6 model (v3 architecture) resulted from a collaboration of Acorn's chip design team with Apple Computer and VLSI Technology. The chip was released in 1992.

The next generation ARM7 was produced in silicon by early 1994. It had a faster multiplier unit, and could operate at lower voltages. Texas Instruments implemented the ARM core in their TMS370 processor line, and augmented the architecture with digital signal processing extensions.

The architecture of the ARM600 processor was driven in part by Apple's requirements. It had a 32-bit address bus, and supported virtual memory. The hardware was optimized for applications that are both price and power sensitive. The processor supported both a user and a supervisor mode. Not a Harvard design, the ARM caches data and instructions together on-chip. However, it has a 64-way set associative cache with 256 lines of 4 words each. The cache was virtual, and the MMU must be enabled for caching to become effective. A settable bit allows the I/O space to be marked as not-cachable. The chip's heritage in RISC and embedded applications give it a fast interrupt response and good code density. A fully static design allowed a slow-down or power-down with no loss of state. This is a critical factor in battery-powered equipment. The ARM architecture is load/store with no memory reference instructions. The load/store operand is a register (32-bit) or an immediate constant. These operations may specify operand increment or decrement, pre- or post- operation. There is a load/store-multiple feature, essentially a block data transfer, but it affects interrupt response, because it is not interuptable. A three-operand format is used. The hardware includes a barrel shifter that one operand always goes through. A barrel shifter is a combinatorial circuit that takes no clock cycles for its operation. The instruction execution process used a 3-stage pipeline.

Although the instruction encoding only allows 16 registers to be used for addresses, the instruction format allows for a complete orthogonal encoding of ALU operations. An integer multiply/accumulate instruction is included. The instruction encoding, which is very "microcode" like, gives a very large number of possible instruction cases, given the conditional execution feature. Floating point operations are not supported in the core, nor is out-of-order execution. A processor provided a complete generic coprocessor interface for up to 16 devices. A floating point coprocessor was designed by ARM Ltd, and built by Plessey. Now, ARM units including floating point internally.

The chip uses a Von Neumann architecture, with one address space. Data path width was 32-bits, with a 26-bit address on the 610 and earlier processors, expanding to a 32-bit address on the 620 and subsequent. A write buffer is included, with space for two pending writes of up to 8 words. When used with the write-thru cache, this feature allows the processor to avoid waiting for external memory writes to complete.

Reset initialization provides for the execution of NOP's when activated, and going to the reset vector address when deactivated. JTAG debugging support was provided in the ARM600 and ARM61O. Request lines for two interrupts were included. The ARM60 was a CMOS Macrocell, available as a VHDL model.

All ARM instructions of the ten basic types are 32 bits in size. An interesting feature is that all instructions are conditionally executable - not just the branches. This means that the programmer does not need to conditionally branch over instructions - the instruction itself is conditional. This feature is under program control via setting of the S-bit. Conditions for execution include the cases always and never. Instructions have 3 operand references, 2 source and 1 destination. Integer math operations include add, subtract, and multiply. No floating point instructions were provided in the baseline architecture. Load/Store operations provide memory access, and a block transfer is provided, that can be aborted. There are AND and XOR logical operations, as well as bit clears and compares. Flow control is accomplished by branch, and branch and link. A software interrupt mechanism provides for supervisor service calls.

The ARM architecture provided visibility and use of the twenty-seven 32-bit registers. The ARM620 had 37 32-bit registers in 6 overlapping sets, and 6 modes of operation. Sixteen registers were visible to the user, the rest being reserved for internal uses, such as the program counter. The state of the general purpose registers at reset time is unknown. Although the registers are general purpose, register 15 is the program counter. This has some advantages and disadvantages. If we use R15 as the destination of an ALU operation, we get a type of indirect branch for free. However, this approach doesn't support delayed branches, which require two program counters for a short while.

Register 14 holds the return address for calls, and is shadowed in all cases. The stack pointer is generally held in Register 13, with Register 12 being used for stack frame pointer. The stack pointer points to the last stacked item. With each stack push operation, the SP is decremented, and the item is put on the stack. Interrupts and the supervisor mode have private stack pointers and link registers.

In terms of byte ordering, the 610 was little-endian, but the 620 could operate in little- or big- endian mode. Supported data types included bytes and 32-bit words. Development support included an ANSI c compiler and run-time libraries, an assembler with linker and librarian, a floating point emulator package, symbolic debugger, and instruction set emulator. Hardware evaluation and prototyping cards were available for the pc bus, and as a platform-independent, stand-alone unit.

The ARM Cortex processors are the latest in the 32-bit series, and extend into multicore and 64-bit models for higher performance. There are three basic models of the Cortex processors, targeting different applications areas. These are provided as licensable products by ARM, Ltd., and produced by multiple chip manufacturers.

NEON implements an advanced SIMD instruction set and was first introduced with the ARM Cortex –A8 model. This is an extension of the FPU with a quad Multiply-and-Accumulate (MAC) unit and additional 64-bit and 128-bit registers.

The Cortex-A8 is a superscalar architecture, with dual instruction issue. The NEON SIMD unit is optional, as is floating point support. The architecture supports Thumb-2 and Jazelle, but only single core. Advanced branch prediction algorithms provide an accuracy rate reportedly approaching 95%. Up to a four megabyte Level-2 cache is provided. There is a 128-bit SIMD engine. Cortex A-8 chips have been implemented by Samsung, TI, and Freescale, among others.

The Cortex-A9 can have multiple cores that are multi-issue superscalar and support out-of-order and speculative execution using register renaming. It has an 8-stage pipeline. Two instructions per cycle can be decoded. There are up to 64k of 4-way set associative Level-1 cache, with up to 512k of Level 2. A 64-bit Harvard architecture memory access allows for maximum bandwidth. Four doubleword writes take five machine cycles. Floating point units and a media processing engine are available for each core. The Cortex-A supports the Thumb-2 instructions.

The ARM Cortex-R has specific features to address performance in real-time applications. These include an instruction cache and a data cache, a floating point coprocessor, and an extended 8-stage pipeline. Cortex-R supports the Thumb and Thumb-2 instructions as well as ARM. Up to 64-bit data structures are supported. The compiler must be aware of which architecture is used as the code target, to introduce the proper optimizations for the various models. As with different implementations of the ISA-32 instruction set from Intel, different implementation architectures require different optimization strategies. The correct optimization for an AMD chip could be the worst-case approach for a pure Intel implementation.

Cortex M addresses microcontrollers. There are currently four models, the Cortex-M0, 1, 2, and 3. All are binary compatible. The M0 and M1 are based on the ARMv6, the M3 is based on the ARMv7, and the M4 is based on the ARM-V7-ME. The Thumb and Thumb-2 subsets are supported. The M3 model has a single cycle 32x32 hardware multiply and 10-12 cycle hardware divide instruction. The M4 adds Digital Signal Processing instructions such as a single-cycle 16/32 bit multiply-accumulate, and supports full Thumb and Thumb-2 instruction set. The IEEE-754 floating point unit is included with the M4. A nested, vectored interrupt controller is included. The 256 interrupts are fully deterministic, and an NMI is included. Cortex-M does not support the instruction and data caches, or the coprocessor interface, and has only a 3-stage pipeline. Only the M3 and M4 models support the Memory Protection Unit. The M3 instruction set provides a pair of synchronization primitives for a guaranteed atomic read-modify-write operation, which is critical to real-time operating systems.

Intergraph Clipper

The Clipper architecture was developed by Fairchild Semiconductor in 1985. The chip was fabricated by Integraph Corp. in 1987, targeted to high end UNIX graphics workstations. There were 3 models: the C100, the C300, and the C400. The planned C-500 did not get implemented. The Clipper featured 8 pipelines and was a Harvard architecture. It had 4k of I-cache and 4k of D-cache. It supported floating point, and had MMU/cache management in a separate chip.

Hardware scoreboarding was implemented, and there were 32 registers. The design achieved single-cycle execution with a load/store approach, and a relatively small instruction set (100). However, the variable length instructions were not very risc-like, nor was the multiple addressing modes. There was no support for out-of-order execution.

ntergraph C4, photo courtesy CPUShack, John Culver.

The C500 was to be superscalar and superpipelined (4 stage), capable of 2 instruction issues per clock, and with 64-bit wide data paths. The architecture was dropped in 1993 in favor of commodity chips from Intel and Sparc.

Hobbit

The Hobbit was AT&T's 32-bit risc architecture to addresses the personal communicator market. The goal was to maximize mips/watt.

The 92010 processor was derived from the earlier CRISP architecture, with hardware optimized to run the c language, and achieved better than 1 instruction per cycle. There were 44 instructions, but no load or store, it was a memory to memory architecture. There was a 256 byte stack cache on the CPU chip. Un-risc-like, there were 7 operand addressing modes.

The 92011 system management chip included the system clock, interrupt controller, dram control and a serial port. The system allowed for up to 5 bus masters.

The 92012 was a pcmcia controller; the 92013 was a peripheral controller for the ISA bus, and the 92014 was a video controller for LCD or CRT screens.

The Hobbit featured single cycle instructions with a pipeline and decoded instruction cache. Operand bypassing in the pipeline was supported.

Branch folding was supported, a technique where a branch is folded back into a previous instruction. The program counter was not incremented, but gets the target address instead. This produces a zero-cycle branch.

IA-32/64

The Instruction Set Architecture, 32 bits, (IA-32) forms the basis for Intel's chips from the 80386 to the Pentium IV and beyond. The earlier Intel processors were 8 or 16 bits. This architecture was extended to 32 bits in the 80386 and would be extended to 64 bits later.

IA-32 features variable length instructions (which are a challenge to pipeline), a small number of registers, multiple, complicated instruction modes. It is then a CISC, not a RISC architecture. In later models, it would be recognized the instruction set had reached its limits of optimization, and dynamic instruction translation to an internal risc instruction set for execution would be used. The CISC instruction set did provide support for legacy code, which was an important issue for Intel.

Pentium was a superscalar design, and the Nx586, PentiumPro, and AMD K5 translated x86 instructions into RISC-like instructions dynamically for execution on a superscalar implementation.

The Pentium IV issued 6 instructions per clock cycle into a 20 stage pipeline. However, these were not 80x86 instructions. They were RISC instructions, that the 80x86 instructions had been dynamically translated into. This approach was used for subsequent x86 architecture chips; x86 on the outside, RISC on the inside.

Other company's implemented the X-86 ISA into their chips under license from Intel. AMD took the basic architecture and added techniques for optimization from their 29k risc chip to produce the x-86 compatible K5 chip. Their follow-on K6 had a RISC86 core, with instruction translation. Next, the Athlon incorporated 3 integer, 3 floating point, and 3 address calculation pipelines. The integer pipes were 10-stage, and the floating was 15-stage.

Cyrix used the ISA-32 with register renaming and speculative execution. NexGen featured the dynamic translation of the 80x86 instructions into internal 104-bit RISC instructions. WinChip implemented branch prediction in the x86.

The Motorola PowerPC-615 could execute PowerPC or IA-32 instructions, by translation, The Toshiba Tigershark could translate IA-32 instructions to SPARC format, dynamically.

The 64-bit x86 machines use more advanced optimization techniques. An HP/Intel design used VLIW (Very Long Instruction Words) to contain 3 instructions in 128 bits. Techniques in instruction-level parallelism include superscalar implementations and instruction re-ordering in hardware.

The Intel Atom CPU is an x86 architecture optimized for low power. It was introduced in 2008, and is now available in multicore and hyper-threaded editions, with speeds beyond 2 GHz. It translates x86 instructions into internal RISC instructions on the fly, and can execute two integer instructions per clock.IMS6250
International Meta Systems, in 1986, came up with a unique architecture that provided hardware emulation for both the Intel 80x86 and the Motorola 680x0. It featured regular instruction encoding and length, with single cycle execution. It used microcode for emulation. The risc core was dual issue superscalar, with a 4-stage pipeline. The native risc instructions were 3-operand. There were 32-bit instructions, all single-cycle except the multiply. There was no floating point hardware support. The chip included an on-chip register file.
On March 2, 1998, International Meta Systems, Inc. filed a voluntary petition for reorganization under Chapter 11 in the U. S. Bankruptcy Court for the Western District of Texas in Austin.

MIPS

Meaning "microprocessor without interlocking stages," the MIPS architecture was the brainchild of John Hennessy at Stanford University. It was produced by multiple manufacturers, and addressed the workstation market. MIPS, the company, was the first to ship a commercial RISC processor, in 1985. The company was eventually bought by SGI. MIPS was the keeper of the architectural specification of the chips, with various company's producing variants.

There were several architectural models of the MIPS chip. The R-2000 was a 32-bit load/store machine with associated MMU and floating point chips. There were 32 registers, with R0=0, and R31 the link address for a branch. The R-3000 was also 32-bit, and was produced in various versions for the embedded market. The R-4000 was a 64-bit machine with integral coprocessors.

The R-2000 chip was an integer CPU with a 5-stage pipeline, and 32 32-bit registers. Register zero was defined as zero, and Register 31 contained a return address. All instructions were a standard 32-bits in length for ease of decode and pipelining. The architecture allowed for 1 to 4 coprocessors, tightly coupled. CR0 was defined as the system control processor, the mmu. CR1 was the floating point processor. The five-stage pipeline included stations for fetch, decode, ALU, memory access, and write. The compiler was responsible for inserting a NOP instruction after any instruction using the results of a previous instruction. This is the "no interlocking stages" part.

The 1988 R-3000 processor was a Harvard architecture internally, having separate data and instruction paths. It supported multiprocessing. There was an associated R-3010 floating point coprocessor. The floating point unit had its own set of 32 x 32-bit registers, and used a 6-stage pipeline. The R3000 had an integral 64-entry translation lookaside buffer. Many embedded variations of the R-3000 architecture were produced.

The 1994 R-4000 was a true 64-bit chip, with 64-bit address bus, registers, ALU, and data paths. It was a dual-issue, 8-stage pipeline design. The later R-6000 was implemented in very fast yet power-hungry ECL technology.

The MIPS architecture was bi-endian, supporting both little-endian or big-endian mode, selectable at reset.

Hewlett-Packard HP-PA

The PA part of the chip's name refers to Hewlett-Packard's Precision Architecture, a RISC approach that was introduced in 1986. HP abandoned the PA in favor of the joint project with Intel which resulted in the Itanium architecture, which was not RISC.

The PA architecture had 32 32-bit registers, and 16 64-bit registers.

Later, the number of floating point registers was increased to 32. The chips use a large Level-1 cache, but most have no Level-2 cache. The family also incorporated SIMD instructions. In 1996, the architecture was extended to 64 bits, as PA-RISC 2.0. The symmetric multiprocessing PA-8800 was two PA cores on a single chip. There were on-chip L1 Harvard, and off-chip L2 caches.

PIC

PIC is a large family of Harvard architecture microcontrollers made by Microchip Technology, derived from the PIC1650 originally developed by General Instrument's Microelectronics Division. The name PIC initially referred to "Peripheral Interface Controller".

The PIC architecture is characterized by a separate code and data spaces (Harvard architecture) for devices other than PIC32, which has a Von Neumann architecture. It has a small number of fixed length instructions, with most instructions being single cycle execution (2 clock cycles, or 4 clock cycles in 8 bit models), with one delay cycle on branches and skips. There is one accumulator (W0), the use of which as source operand is implied (i.e. is not encoded in the opcode), All RAM locations function as registers for both source and destination of math and other functions. A hardware stack is used for storing return addresses. A fairly small amount of addressable data space is provided which can be extended through memory banking. The program counter is mapped into the data space and writable (this is used to implement indirect jumps).

In the PIC18 series, the program memory is addressed in 8-bit increments (bytes), which differs from the instruction width of 16-bits.

There is no distinction between memory space and register space because the RAM comprises both memory and registers, and the RAM is usually just referred to as the register file or simply as the registers.

PICs have a set of registers that function as general purpose RAM. Special purpose control registers for on-chip hardware resources are also mapped into the data space. The addressability of memory varies depending on device series, and all PIC devices have some banking mechanism to extend addressing to additional memory. Later series of devices feature move instructions which can cover the whole addressable space, independent of the selected bank. In earlier devices, any register move had to be achieved via the accumulator.

External data memory is not directly addressable except in some high pin count PIC18 devices. The code space is generally implemented as ROM, EPROM or flash ROM. In general, external code memory is not directly addressable due to the lack of an external memory interface. The exceptions are PIC17 and select high pin count PIC18 devices. 8-bit chunks. However, the unit of addressability of the code space is not generally the same as the data space. For example, PICs in the baseline and mid-range families have program memory addressable in the same word size as the instruction width, i.e. 12 or 14 bits respectively. In contrast, in the PIC18 series, the program memory is addressed in 8-bit increments (bytes), which differs from the instruction width of 16 bits, which makes them hard to characterize.

PICs have a hardware call stack, which is used to save return addresses. The hardware stack is not software accessible on earlier devices, but this changed with the 18 series devices.

A PIC's instruction set varies from about 35 instructions for the low-end PICs to over 80 instructions for the high-end units. The instruction set includes operations on registers directly, on the accumulator and a literal constant, on the accumulator and a register, and for conditional execution, and program branching.

Some operations, such as bit setting and testing, can be performed on any numbered register, but bi-operand arithmetic operations always involve W (the accumulator), writing the result back to either W or the other operand register. To load a constant, it is necessary to load it into W before it can be moved into another register. On the older cores, all register moves needed to pass through W, but this changed on the "high end" cores.

PIC cores have skip instructions which are used for conditional execution and branching. The skip instructions are 'skip if bit set' and 'skip if bit not set'. Because cores before PIC18 had only unconditional branch instructions, conditional jumps are implemented by a conditional skip (with the opposite condition) followed by an unconditional branch. Skips are also of utility for conditional execution of any immediate single following instruction.

The architectural decisions of PIC are directed at the maximization of speed-to-cost ratio. The PIC architecture was among the first scalar CPU designs and is still among the simplest and cheapest. The Harvard architecture—in which instructions and data come from separate sources—simplifies timing and microcircuit design greatly, and this benefits clock speed, price, and power consumption.

The PIC architectures have a small, easy to learn instruction set. They have a built in oscillator with selectable speeds, and feature in-circuit programming plus in circuit debugging. There is a wide range of I/O interfaces including I2C, SPI, USB, USART, A/D, programmable comparators, PWM, LIN, CAN, PSP, and Ethernet. The PIC architectures do have several limitations, including only a single accumulator. Register-bank switching is required to access the entire RAM of many devices. Operations and registers are not orthogonal; some instructions can address RAM and/or immediate constants, while others can only use the accumulator.

The hardware call stack is not addressable, so preemptive task switching cannot be implemented. Software-implemented stacks are not efficient, so it is difficult to generate reentrant code and support local variables.

An example of a contemporary 8-bit soft core, instantiated in an FPGA, is the SpaceRISC8 Microcontroller, which has the instruction set of the PIC16F86 chip, from Microchip Technology, Inc.

SH7000

The SH7000 risc chips by Hitachi was used in the SEGA game system, and embedded control. It had 16-bit instructions; most were single cycle. There were 16 registers for general purpose use, and the architecture was pipelined. It included Digital Signal Processing (DSP) functionality. The architecture was load/store. Originally the chips had no floating point support nor MMU. There were multiple addressing modes, and the design was pipelined.

The SuperH architecture is a 32-bit ISA design from Hitachi. It is targeted to embedded systems, and was begun in the early 1990's. The 16-bit SH-1 and SH-2 models found application in game consoles such as the Sega. The SH-2 has 16 general purpose registers, and instructions are fixed length, with a five stage pipeline. The SH-2 was extended to the superscalar SH-2A. The SH-3 model had memory management, as well as a DSP extension. The SH-4 model was used in the SEGA Dreamcast console in 1998. This unit was 2-way superscalar, and included a vector floating point unit. It had four floating point multiply units, and incorporated interrupt and dma support, and power management features. The SH-5 was a 64-bit design, with dual modes. The compact mode is SH-4 compatible. The media mode has 32-bit instructions, with sixty-four 64-bit data registers. Instructions can be SIMD. Branch prefetching is supported.

SPARC

The Scalable Processor Architecture (SPARC) is an open architecture, based on Patterson's Berkeley RISC. In contrast to the specification level of the MIPS processor, SPARC processors are instruction set compatible, and may be hardware compatible. In addition, the Bus specification and the reference MMU specification are usually adhered to by implementers. Multiple vendors support SPARC in different technologies. By early 1991, over 36 SPARC implementations were in existence, from at least 8 vendors.

The Cypress 7C601 early implementation of the basic Version 7 specification was typical, and provided fixed length instructions, a load/store model, hard-wired decoding of instructions, and single clock execution, achieved by pipelining. The integer, floating point, and memory management units were separate in this implementation. A four-stage pipeline was used, with 6 to 32 overlapping register windows. Each window featured 8 global and 24 local 32-bit wide registers, with 6 control registers. A single length load was a two-cycle instruction, while a single store was a three-cycle instruction. A branch was a one or two cycle instruction. An annul bit was used for conditional branches. The load/store operations could be done on byte, half-word, word, and double-word items.

Fifty simple instructions were provided, with support for 128 different hardware and software traps and exceptions. Memory protection included a user and a supervisor mode. The four stages of the pipeline were: operand code (opcode) fetch, decode/operand read, execute, and writeback.

The SPARC architecture relied on the register window architecture, which provides a hardware mechanism for procedure calling, reduces access to memory, and is configurable for fast context switching. As technology improved more set of register windows were provided.

Exception handling depended on whether an internal or external event is occurring. An internal event is synchronous, and response is immediate, where the currently executing instruction is aborted before the processor changes state. An external event, occurring asynchronously, allowed the currently executing to complete. Interrupt latency ranges from 3-7 cycles.

The SPARC memory management scheme included an address space identifier bit field, which identified the memory access types as user or supervisor instruction or data fetches (4 types).

The 7C602 floating point unit from Cypress semiconductor added single and double precision floating point performance to the integer processor. It featured its own register files, and internal 64 bit data paths. It was synchronous in operation with the integer processor.

The SPARC reference MMU specifies a 32 bit virtual to 36 bit physical address space translation, with support for multiple contexts, and page level protection mechanisms.

Cypress' implementation was the 7C604 CMU, which implemented the reference MMU, plus cache tag and control, and Mbus control into one device. It featured a 4k byte page size, 64 fully associative lockable TLB entries. It implemented memory address protection checking, and 4096 contexts. The cache controller handled 2k direct-mapped virtual cache tag entries, and had a write-through and a copy-back mode. The 32-byte cache size allowed for 8 instructions to be cached. It could be locked, and featured alias detection in hardware. It used burst mode access to main memory. Multiple CMU's could be used in a system, which expanded the cache size and the number of TLB entries.

SPARC V8 (1990) introduced integer multiply and divide hardware, and quad-precision floating point. The various functional units of the V7 architecture were combined on a single chip. It also became an IEEE standard, 1754-1994. The SPARC architecture is licensed to a large number of companies, who build various chips. SPARC V9 is the 64-bit extension to the architecture, released in 1993.

SPARC in Space
The ERC32 is a radiation-tolerant 32-bit RISC SPARC V7 processor for space applications. It was developed by Temic (now Atmel) for the European Space Agency. Two versions were manufactured, the ERC32 Chip Set (Part Names: TSC691, TSC692, TSC693), and the ERC32 Single Chip (Part Name: TSC695). These implementations follow SPARC V7 specifications. Cache and MMU functions are not included.

Implementations went from a 3-chip set in the 1990's to a single chip version by the end of the decade. Support for the chipset version of the ERC32 has been discontinued. The LEON processor is the follow-on, and supports the SPARC V8 specification.

The LEON project was started by the European Space Agency (ESA) in late 1997 to develop a high-performance processor. It was to be an open, portable, and non-proprietary processor design, capable of meeting future requirements for performance, software compatibility, and low system cost. To maintain correct operation in the presence of single event upsets (SEU's), extensive error detection and error handling functions were needed.

All processors in the LEON series are based on the SPARC-V8 RISC architecture. LEON2 has a five-stage pipeline while later versions have a seven-stage pipeline. LEON2 and LEON2-FT are distributed as system-on-chip designs. The standard LEON2 includes an interrupt controller, debug support hardware, 24-bit timers, a UART, a 16-bit I/O port, and a memory controller.

Transmeta Crusoe

The Crusoe chips was IA-32 (Intel x86) compatible, and targeted the low power (mobile devices) market. It used code morphing, a technique that traded hardware for software to improve speed. The company was founded in 1985, and the chip was introduced in Jan 2000.

The chip dynamically translated x86 instructions to VLIW (very long instruction word) format. This was accomplished by a software layer, residing in flash rom. It included a translation cache.

There were four models of the chip, each with 128 kbytes cache. The chip achieved compatibility with existing software, while providing a low power, low heat approach. This facilitated battery powered devices, as well as densely packed servers. Transmeta's metric was performance/per watt/per cubic foot.

Following the Crusoe was the Efficeon, a Pentium-4 class machine, with a power consumption of several watts. The Efficeon had two arithmetic logic units, dual load/store/add units, two execute units, two floating-point/MMX/SSE/SSE2 units, a branch prediction unit, and a control unit. The VLIW core could execute one 256-bit VLIW instruction per clock cycle. The VLIW word could store eight 32-bit instructions. Linus Torvalds, of Linux fame, worked for Transmeta at one time.

V800

The V800 chip was introduced by NEC in 1992, targeted to the PDA and game markets. It included a 5 stage pipeline, and single-cycle instructions. It had a large (32 element) register file, a single addressing mode, and was load/store. There were 89 instructions in two lengths (16 and 32 bits), and no MMU. The chips included a barrel shifter and a hardware multiplier. The design included bit string instructions, which are risc-pathological. It was a fully static design; the clock could be slowed or stopped with no data loss. The chips could address up to 4 gigabytes of memory, and on-chip caches were included. The design was proprietary to NEC. Standard parts are still available, as are IP cores.

Internal RAM and ROM were provided in some models, and external memory could be used. I/O was memory mapped.

iWarp

The iWarp was a parallel supercomputer project, designed by Carnegie Mellon University and implemented in silicon by Intel. The architecture of the computing nodes was very close to the Transputer model. The first Intel-produced chips were delivered to CMU in 1990. The cpu was 32-bits in size, and had a 64-bit floating point unit. The main alu executed one instruction per cycle at a clock rate of 20 MHz. Included with the computation units were four serial channels, able to operate as 20 virtual channels. They did not include memory on the chips. Four iWarp chips were installed on a board, and a system consisted of 64 cpu's connected in an 8x8 torus configuration.

Transputer

The Transputer was a chip too far ahead of its time. Update the clock speeds, and the architecture would be impressive today. It was a microcomputer, having a cpu, memory, and I/O on one chip. The external logic required was minimal. Large arrays of Transputer's were easily implemented. However, like many advanced technological artifacts, it was hard to understand and apply. It took a while to get used to the software approach. The tools were difficult to use. In fact, the software approach, the conceptual model, was what made the Transputer powerful. The implementation in silicon came later. You had to understand and buy into the conceptual model and then the software to maximize your return from the Transputer. A steep learning curve was involved. In the end, the Transputer was overtaken by simpler, better-funded, mainstream approaches.

The Inmos Transputer architecture was introduced in 1985 as a single chip microcomputer architecture, optimized for parallel use in Multiple Instruction, Multiple Data (MIMD) configurations. It provided excellent and balanced interprocessor communications as well as computational ability. Transporter's provided the capability to implement scalable systems. Timers were included internally, and the chip required only a crystal to derive its own clock. The timers enabled real time programming and process scheduling. Because the input clock was 5 MHz regardless of the internal rate of the Transputer, a master clock could be distributed across a board.

The architecture of the Transputer from Inmos Corporation can best be understood by looking at the origins of the device. The Transputer family was a British design. In essence, the Transputer implemented in hardware the parallel language Occam. Emphasis was placed on communicating between processes as well as computational ability. To understand the Transputer architecture you have to understand Occam, and communicating parallel processes. However, to use the Transputer, you could program in C, Pascal, Fortran, or several other familiar languages. Occam remained a barrier to widespread acceptance of the Transputer, but it matched the hardware.

Since the introduction of the Transputer in 1985, the unit went on to be the world leader in number of units shipped for any RISC processor in 1989 and 1990. By the end of 1990, over 1/2 million Transputer units had been shipped, which translated into a large installed base, even considering that a large number of units went into embedded applications.

Inmos had been founded by the British Government in 1978. Inmos was purchased by Thorn EMI, and was later was sold to SGS-Thompson. A military products line provided Transputer family parts in compliance with MIL-STD-883. As single chip microcontrollers, Transputers have flown on space missions.

As controllers, Transputers provided an excellent approach, as they included cpu, memory, and I/O in one package. A minimum of external components was required for systems. Using their unique interprocessor communication architecture, Transputers were the ideal building block for parallel systems.

The Transputer processor family consisted of the 16-bit T222 and T225, and the 32-bit T400, T414, T800, T801, and T805. The T400 series of Transputers included 32-bit integer processors, 4 kbytes of internal memory, and four high-speed serial links. The T-800 family added an integral 64-bit floating-point processor in 1987. The T-9000 series expanded the capabilities of the device by a factor of 10 in computation and communication.

The T-801 Transputer was a variation of the T-800 with a non-multiplexed address/data bus. Thus, the package size (i.e., pin count) was larger than the standard T-800. It was easier to interface directly with external static memory than the T-800. The T-805 was a T-800 with some additional debug instructions, and with several additional control signals to ease the design of dynamic memory systems in a dma environment. In addition, the T805 had support for 2-dimensional graphics via a new set of instructions, and CRC calculations on arbitrary length data streams. Multiplexed data and address lines were used.

The M212 was a special purpose Transputer device for peripheral control. It was a derivative of the T2 16-bit architecture, with specific interface logic for disk drives. It allowed disk drives to become nodes on a network of link-connected Transputers.

The Transputer featured high speed interconnect by means of full duplex asynchronous serial communications. Associated communication interface devices included the C011 and C012, which interfaced parallel data transfers to the two-wire link protocol. The C004 device was a 32 x 32 crossbar switch for links. The C004 was fully programmable, dynamically switchable, and controlled by a link interface.

In addition to the general purpose T-800 series, Inmos manufactured a series of special purpose processor units. These included the A-100 Cascadable Signal Processor, the A-110 Image and Signal Processing subsystem, the A-121 2-D discrete cosine transform image processor, and the STI3220 Motion Estimation Processor.

The follow-on processor to the T-800 was announced by Inmos in April 1991, and was called the T-9000. This unit was code-compatible with existing T-800 units, but provided an order-of-magnitude performance increase in both computational and communication capability. The unit incorporated a 32-bit integer processor, 64-bit floating-point processor, 16 kilobytes of internal memory, four upgraded I/O links, and two configuration links on a single chip. In addition, the interrupt and memory interface were improved. The new computer chip was accompanied by the C-104 packet routing chip, and the C-100 system protocol converter, which translated between T-800 class link communication, and the T-9000 scheme. The T-9000 appeared in Spring, 1993. There were rumors of a follow-on 0.5 micron processor code named E1.

The T-9000 chip maintained binary code compatibility with the T-800, and could be mixed in systems with the earlier processor. However, both the internal processor instruction rate and the link communication rate had been enhanced. The T-9000 was a superscalar, pipelined architecture, with extensive on-chip cache.

The Transputer's four kilobyte on-chip ram could be allocated for cache, data, or instructions, and simple programs executing entirely from on-chip ram were very fast. Four kilobytes may not seem like a lot of space, but instructions were one byte. On-chip ram provided single-cycle access, while external memory was a minimum of three-cycle access.

Instead of having a large number of registers on the chip, the Transputer was a stack machine. This provided for a very fast task context switch for interrupt response and task switching. The three-deep operand stack corresponds to the 3-address instruction format of other processors. The transistors, or silicon real estate normally used for scoreboarded registers was devoted to on-chip fast static ram, which could be used for code, data, or stack space. The external memory space was spanned by 32 address bits, and was addressed in a flat model. The internal memory provides a fast access workspace. Only workspace and instruction pointers were saved in a context switch. For interrupts, the three stack registers also need to be saved. The workspace pointer register locates the local variables in memory. Transputers access words, except for byte and Boolean arrays.

The Transputer could boot from ROM, or from a link, selectable by the state of a data pin. Booting from link allowed for fast initialization of a large collection of interconnected Transputers.

i960

The Intel i960 was a 32-bit RISC embedded processor family dating from 1984. They were not code-compatible with other Intel products. They featured 32, 32-bit register, with a priority interrupt controller, on-chip instruction cache (1k to 16k), with data cache (1k to 8k) on some models, a PCI controller, and a memory controller on chip. Some models included dual 32-bit timers and an i2c bus. They were a superscalar architecture with register scoreboarding. Some models had an integral IEEE-754 floating point unit.

42

The processor is still in use for selected military applications. It's design was influenced by the iAPX432 project at Intel, and the i960 design was a joint effort with Siemens. In order not to compete with its own i860 and i386 products in the general purpose computing market, Intel targeted the i960 to the embedded market.

The i960 followed the Berkeley school of RISC design, with register windows and fast subroutine calls. The memory space was flat.

i860

Intel's i860 was called "a Cray on a chip" when it was introduced. The i860 addressed the high-end graphics and computation enhancement markets. There were two members of the i860 family, the XR and the XP. The i860 processor achieved high levels of integer, floating point, and 3D graphics performance simultaneously. The i860XR was a pure 64-bit risc design at the 1 million transistor level, using 1 micron, double metal processes in CHMOS. The i860XR achieved the same scalar performance and one fourth to one half of the vector performance of the first Cray machine, which is now in the Smithsonian. The era of the desktop supercomputer had arrived. It's superscalar architecture allowed up to 3 instructions/clock to be executed. The on-chip 8k data and 4k instruction caches had very high bandwidth due to wide internal data paths. The caches were two-way set-associative, and utilized a write-back scheme. The instruction cache's data path was 64-bits, while the data cache's was 128-bits. The chip's external data bus was 64-bits in width, but secondary cache was not supported. The chip was a Harvard architecture internally, but with a unified memory architecture externally. Dual instruction mode, in which a 64 bit wide integer and floating point pair is fetched and executed similtaneously, is a variation of the long instruction word format. The chip utilized a load/store architecture, with on-chip transfers taking advantage of the wide internal data paths.

Intel's second-generation i860, the XP, extended the edge of the performance envelope a considerable distance using 0.8 micron, triple level CHMOS to achieve a density of 2.5 million transistors. The chip was binary compatible with the previous version, but doubled the performance figures by adding support for second level cache, faster busses, larger on-chip caches, as well as upping the clock speed. Multiprocessing support was added in the form of hardware support for bus snooping for cache consistency, and bus arbitration features.

The integer unit achieved the one instruction per clock goal. Integer register bypassing was available, where the result of an operation was available as an input to the next stage in the pipeline without a register write/read. A single-cycle loop instruction was included. The integer unit could handle loads, stores, and loop control, while the floating point unit did multiplies and adds.

The floating point unit used dedicated 3-stage pipelines for the add and multiply units. The unit supported the data types, operations, and exceptions defined in the IEEE 754 standard format.

The built-in 3D graphics unit also used pipelined techniques to speed up operations, such as management of Z-buffers, and color shading. These techniques were used in shading and hidden line removal algorithms for high performance graphics. Display techniques such as pixel interpolation and Gouraud shading were supported by hardware graphics primitives, high speed floating point multiply, and vectorization of operations. In addition, the graphics unit could add and subtract 64-bit integers.

DMA handshake protocols also provided for multiprocessor bus mastership hand off. A single interrupt pin was provided, and the external interrupt could be masked in software. The i860 mmu design was borrowed from the i386 family. The XR included hardware support for cache consistency, bus snooping, and arbitration.

The i860 bus architecture was Harvard internally, unified externally. Bus width was 64 bits. On- chip write buffers were used.

Upon reset, execution began at the highest memory address. The program initialized control registers, and the caches were flushed, although they were marked as invalidated. Execution began at the supervisor level.

A 1-times clock was used, 25 - 40 MHz for the XR, 40 - 50 MHZ for the XP.

Hardware support for testing was provided in the i860 parts, with a compliance with the IEEE P1149.1/D6 specification, and a test access port (tap).

Second level (external) cache for the XP part was supplied by the companion 82495XP cache controller in conjunction with the 82490XP cache RAM. The secondary cache was unified. Cache write-through was supported.

In the i860 instruction set, all instructions were 32-bits in size, and either a register or a control format. The integer math instructions included add and subtract on up to 32 bit entities. 64 bit integers were handled in the graphics unit. Floating point instructions included add, subtract, multiply, reciprocal, square root, compares and conversions. Pipelined floating operations included add/multiply, subtract/multiply, multiply/add, and multiply/subtract. Load/store operations operated on integer, floating, or pixel items. Left and right shifts were provided, as well as the AND, OR, and XOR logical operations.

Flow control instructions included call subroutine, branch conditional and unconditional, and a software trap instruction. Special graphics instructions supported Z-buffer and pixel operations. The XP provided additional operations for load and store I/O, and cache flush.

On the i860 chips were 32 32-bit integer registers and 32 32-bit floating point registers. R0 was read as zero, as were F0 and F1. There were twelve control registers, including the processor status register (PSR), the floating point status register (FSR), the extended PSR (EPSR), the data breakpoint register (DB), the directory base register, the fault instruction register, the bus error address register, the concurrency control register, and 4 privilege registers P0-P4.

The PSR contained current state information, including condition codes, the loop condition code, a shift count, a pixel size indicator, bits for data access trapping, indicators of interrupt mode and previous interrupt mode, and user/supervisor mode and previous user/supervisor mode. In addition, 5 trap flags were included. The other fields were Delayed Switch, dual instruction mode, and a kill-next-floating-point instruction.

The EPSR contained more information about the state, including the processor type and stepping number (manufacturing variation), endian setting, on-chip data cache size, bus error flag, overflow flag, trap indicators for delayed instruction, auto increment, and pipeline usage, a write-protect bit for the directory and page table entries, and interlock bit for trap sequences.

The floating point status register contained information about the current state of the floating point processor, including rounding modes, trap status, overflow and underflow from the adder or multiplier, and trap enables. The data breakpoint register stored the breakpoint address if a trap was taken. The Directory base register was used to control caching, address translation and bus options. It contained the 20 high order bits of the page directory, the fields for the cache replacement/flushing control, a bus lock bit, a virtual address enable, a DRAM page size indicator, and a code size bit, to allow bootstrapping from 8 bit wide devices. The fault instruction register was used to hold the address of the instruction causing a trap. Similarly, the bus error address register held the address for the bus cycle during which a bus error or parity error was detected. The concurrency control register was used to enable or disable the concurrency control feature for multiprocessing, and to specify the controlled address space.
Byte ordering was selectable in software, with the normal mode being little-endian. The controlling bit was contained in the extended PSP register.

In the i860, most data types were compatible with those of the 80x86 family. Data types included 8- to 64-bit integers, and 32-, 64-, or 128-bit floating point operands. The i860XP pixel processor operated on 8-, 16-, or 32-bit data items. In a 16-bit wide pixel, there were 6 bits of intensity for red and green, and 5 bits for blue. The 32-bit format had 8 bits for each color, plus 8 bits for general use.

Floating point was the i860 architecture's strong point, with double precision adds taking 3 cycles, and double precision multiplies, four. A pipelined mode for vectorized operations allowed one result per cycle (after latency). The adder and multiplier could operate simultaneously. Hardware support for square root and reciprocal were provided. The floating point unit had its own set of 32 registers. IEEE format was supported. All four rounding modes of the IEEE standard were supported. There was no divide operation per se, but a reciprocal and a square root were calculated by Newton-Raphson techniques. In dual mode, an add/subtract and a multiply could be done in parallel.

The 860XR cache was 2-way set associative, and included 4 kbytes for instruction, and 8 kbytes for data. Caches were virtually mapped.

The 860XP used 4-way set associative 16k byte internal instruction and data caches. Both virtual and physical tags were kept. The MESI protocol was supported for multiprocessor cache consistency. The 860XP MMU was extended to add a 4 Megabyte page size. Compatibility with paged 32-bit addressing on the 386/486 model was maintained. The external datapath remained 64-bits in width with posted writes, a three stage read pipeline, and a one-clock burst bus. New control registers were added to support multiprocessing and other operating system functions. Write-back and write-through policies were selectable for the on-chip I- and D- caches.

The on-chip MMU was based on the i80386 design, and provided two level paging, and 4k page size. User and Supervisor mode protection was provided. The mmu used a 64-entry TLB that was 4-way set associative. Hardware support was provided for TLB miss exceptions. On the XP, there was an additional 4 megabyte page size, dynamically selectable. Address translation could be enabled or disabled, and I/O occupied a separate space. The page table included bits for present, writable, user/supervisor, write-thru, cacheable, accessed, and dirty.

Motorola 88000

The Motorola 88000 was a RISC design from the late 1980's, following the MIPS and SPARC designs. It was a 32-bit machine, with a register-register architecture, and supported both little-endian and big-endian data. It had separate instruction and data caches. An external memory management unit, the 88200, was supplied. The 88110 chip had graphics instructions and floating point support. Some 88k features found their way into the joint Motorola-IBM PowerPC architecture. In embedded use, three 88k's were used to implement the triply modular redundant computer in the F-15 aircraft. Motorola dropped the 88k line in favor of the PowerPC.

IBM RISC

IBM had several approaches to RISC in microprocessors. The architecture of IBM's original minicomputer project, the 801, lead to the ROMP ((IBM) Research Office Products Division) processor in 1982. The ROMP cpu was the basis of the IBM RT/PC desktops. Originally 24-bits, it was later changed to a 32-bit architecture. It had 16 32-bit registers. It was designed with a small (118 opcode) set of simple instructions, and it dated from 1977. 16-bit instructions were used for efficiency, and 32-bit instructions for more complex operations. First commercial silicon was in 1981. Software problems delayed first shipment of systems to 1986. The overly ambitious software architecture included virtualization.

POWER stood for Performance Optimization With Enhanced RISC. This represented an Instruction Set Architecture, which came out of a superscalar design of the late 1970's. The 1990 POWER-1 chipset implementation was known as the RS/6000. The POWER-1 was 2-way superscalar with three execution units. It used a 52-bit virtual address. The memory architecture was big-endian, and there were separate data and instruction caches. POWER-1 was implemented in four chips. In 1993, the Power-2 architecture was released. These chipsets were the basis of the IBM RS/6000 systems. An IBM RS/6000-based processor in the Deep Blue computer triumphed over human chess champion Garry Kasparov.

The two processors of the POWER family were the RIOS I and RIOS II, before the design was blended into the PowerPC. POWER-1 used register renaming and out-of-order execution techniques. The POWER-4 design had dual POWER cores on a single chip. The Power-1 led to a single-chip implementation the RISC Single Chip (RSC), and the RAD6000, a radiation-hardened unit for space applications. The PowerPC architecture was a derivative of the POWER.

The Power-PC architecture resulted from a collaboration between Motorola and IBM. Motorola contributed the 88000 RISC architecture, and IBM threw in parts of the ROMPS, RiscPC, and Power architecture. The result was an architecture designed to challenge the Intel IA-32 and IA-64.

The Power-PC was 3-way superscalar, with separate integer, floating point, and branch processing. It supported out-of-order execution and hardware branch prediction. The memory management unit converted 52-bit virtual addresses to 32-bit physical addresses. The internal cache was a unified structure in the early units, moving to a separate or Harvard cache structure later. Multiple processors were supported. The PowerPC could dynamically re-order the load/store traffic at run time.

From a programmer's point of view, the PowerPC was a load/store architecture. All addressing was register indirect. There was an interruptible string move instruction. There were 32 general purpose integer registers, and 32 floating point registers. Byte ordering was selectable, with big-endian being the default. There were 184 instructions, and both a user and supervisor mode.

The PowerPC 601 was the first-generation part, running from 50-120 Mhz. It had a unified cache of 32 kbytes. The part was used by both Apple computer and IBM. The PowerPC 602 project was to be able to execute both PPC and Intel IA-32 instruction sets. It was never completed. The PowerPC reached 66-300 Mhz clock speeds, and introduced the Harvard cache architecture. The PowerPC 604 ran from 100 to 350 Mhz, and the cache size was 64k.

The PowerPC G3, models 740 and 750, featured dual caches of 32k each. The G4 introduced the AltiVec instructions. These were for multimedia data, similar to Intel's MMX extension. The AltiVec instructions, 160 in number, had their own separate set of 32 registers, each 128-bits wide. The G4 ran at 350 to 1100 Mhz, and went to a 7-stage pipeline.

IBM variants of the architecture included the Power3 which was a 64-bit machine and became the basis for the RS6000 servers, and the Power4, which stretched the operating frequency to 1Ghz. Motorola produced embedded versions of the PPC architecture for the automotive and communications industries. A typical MPC 5xx series embedded part included integrated ram, flash, a timer, serial I/O and A/D functions.

Others

Although the thrust of early Reduced Instruction Set Computing development was enhanced computation that usually found itself in engineering workstations, the market for such endeavors was limited in scope. A much larger market, and, more importantly, a volume market, is found in embedded control. Volume markets are cost driven.

An important concept emerges here: although we usually associate RISC with 32- or even 64-bit machines, this is not necessarily always true. For a counterexample, consider the Microchip PIC, which represents a minimalist 8-bit approach to RISC for embedded control. More importantly, conventional RISC manufacturers, who might produce 50-100,000 units for the workstation market, are finding the multi-million piece embedded systems market appealing.

RCA 1802

53

The 8-bit RCA 1802 was one of the first RISC chips. CDP 1801 was a 2-chip set, circa 1975. It operated at 2MHz, using 5,000 transistors, in CMOS technology. The 1800 series processors from RCA were designed by Joe Weisbecker. The 1801's separate chips represented the ALU and the control unit. The 1801 operated up to 4 MHz. It had 59 instructions. The registers could be viewed as 8 or 16 bits in width.

The 1802 was released by RCA in 1976. It was quite a different architecture than other contemporary CPU's, and was produced in complementary metal oxide semiconductor (CMOS) technology, which is both low-power and radiation resistant, though susceptible to electrostatic discharge. It was also a static logic design, which could operate at a wide range of clock speeds down to zero. The architecture has also been implemented in silicon-on-sapphire technology which greatly improves its radiation hardness. It operated at up to 6.4 MHz.

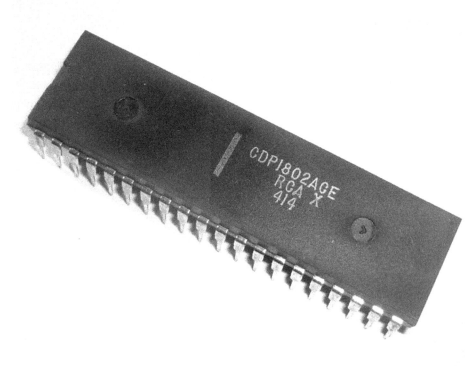

1802's were found in Chrysler Corporation's electronic ignition units for their gas engines, video games, video terminals, the ELF computer. There was a broad family of support chips, including the 1855 multiply/divide coprocessor. The 1804 was an 1802 with 2 KB of ROM and 32 bytes of RAM.

Photo courtesy, cpushack.com

The 1802 had a register file of 16 registers of 16 bits each. Using the SEP instruction, one could select any of the registers to be the program counter or index register. It also used 16-bit addressing. Support chips included the 1852 8-bit I/O port, the 1854 UART, the 1856 memory buffer, and the 1857 I/O buffer.

A few commonly used subroutines could be called quickly by keeping their address in one of the 16 registers. Before a subroutine returned, it jumped to the location immediately preceding its entry point so that after the RET instruction returned control to the caller, the register would be pointing to the right value for next time. An interesting variation was to have two or more subroutines in a ring so that they were called in round-robin order.

EM Microelectronics EM6600 family
These are ultra-lower power microcontrollers available in 8-pin packages, and frequently used for power control. The EM 6882r includes a 4-bit ADC, watchdog timer, PWM, and a 10-bit up/down counter. There are 80 words of 4-bit RAM, and 1536

words of 16-bit ROM. The CPU is RISC-like architecture, with 2 clock cycles per instruction. There are 72 instructions. Included is an 8-bit serial interface. There are 2 external interrupts.

Atmel AVR

AVR makes a modern 8-bit microcontroller in a RISC architecture. It is fully static, meaning the clock can be slowed and stopped, without loss of state. It can operate at 16 MHz, and includes hardware multiplication. There are 130 instructions, and 32 registers. It includes 64 Kbytes of flash memory, and 2 Kbytes of EEPROM, with 4 k bytes of SRAM. It can also address additional external memory. The chip is more than the equivalent of a previous 8-bit generation board.

The AVR includes two 8-bit counter-timers, two 16-bit counter-timers, a real-time counter, dual 8-bit pulse-width modulation registers, up to six 16-bit PWM channels, eight 10-bit ADC's, dual serial UARTS, SPI interface, and an analog comparator. The clock frequency is selectable by software. The AVR is the basis of the popular Arduino microcontroller.

Freescale

The Freescale 68HC16 is a 16-bit follow-on to the earlier 8-bit Motorola 68HC11 microcontroller. The Freescale XGATE is a 16-bit RISC processor derived from the same architecture.

Fujitsu FR series

The Fujitsu RISC refers to a 32-bit family of RISC processors, targeted to embedded applications. Automotive applications are a major target of the architecture. Integral floating point units are provided.

FR processor cores are teamed with the Milbeaut signal processor core on a multicore for image processing applications in high end digital cameras such as Leica and Nikon.

Zilog Z80000

The Zilog 80000 was a 32-bit follow-on to Zilog's Z-8000, Z-800, and Z-80 processors. It was available in 1986. It had a six-stage pipeline, and memory management hardware. It was equivalent in complexity to Intel's 80386. There was a register file of 16 general purpose, variable length registers. It could use the Z8070 floating point c0-processor. It came in a CMOS version, the Z-320.

RISC-DSP

RISC techniques are applicable in special purpose processors beyond integer and floating point. DSP processors, in particular, benefit from the speed-up. In Digital Signal Processing, we are operating on audio or video data with computationally-intensive digital filters.

The key to digital filtering is the Multiply-Accumulate instruction (MAC). Digital filters usually operate on long vectors (single dimension arrays) of data.

One example is Analog Devices' Blackfin extensive series of embedded DSP's. The Blackfin is 32-bit RISC processor with dual 16-bit multiply/accumulate (MAC) units, and provision for 8-bit video processing in real-time. The Blackfin architecture was developed in cooperation with Intel, and announced in 2000. These are derivatives of Analog Device's earlier SHARC architecture and Intel's XScale.

In Blackfin, the DSP part has dual 16-bit MAC units, dual 40-bit ALU's, and a 40-bit barrel shifter. The architecture can execute three instructions per clock. The RISC part has single-cycle instructions, and incorporates data and instruction L1 and L2 caches, as well as on-chip peripherals. It has a memory protection unit, not a memory management unit. Operating systems for the chip can't take advantage of virtual memory. User and Supervisor modes are supported, with an additional emulation mode. The instruction set has 16-, 32-, and 64-bit instructions.

TI's TMS320 series is a family of DSP chips dating from 1983. Some versions use fixed point, and some including floating point capability. The architecture evolved from coprocessor to general purpose cpu's. The architecture is Harvard, separate instruction and data memory, but include the ability to read data from instruction memory. The first generation products were 16-bit. The later C80 product has a 32-bit floating point master processor and four 32-bit fixed point processors. The C2000 series are DSP's with 32-bit microcontrollers (usually ARM). The C5000 series is 16-bit fixed point, with a 6-stage pipeline. These find application in mobile phones.

RISC is not a big deal anymore. It has gone mainstream, and every processor uses some RISC techniques to enhance performance.

Glossary of Terms and Acronyms

1's complement – a binary number representation scheme for negative values.

2's complement – another binary number representation scheme for negative values.

Accumulator – a register to hold numeric values during and after an operation.

ACM – Association for Computing Machinery; professional organization.

Ada – a programming language named after Ada Augusta, Countess of Lovelace, and daughter of Lord Byron; arguably, the first programmer. Collaborator with Charles Babbage.

ALU – arithmetic logic unit.

ANSI – American National Standards Institute

API – application program interface; specification for software modules to communicate.

ArpaNet – Advanced Research Projects Agency (U.S.), first packet switched network, 1968.

ASCII - American Standard Code for Information Interchange, a 7-bit code; developed for teleprinters.

ASIC – application specific integrated circuit, custom or semicustom,.

Assembly language – low level programming language specific to a particular ISA.

Async – asynchronous; using different clocks.

Babbage, Charles –early 19th century inventor of mechanical computing machinery to solve difference equations, and output typeset results; later machines would be fully programmable.

Barrel shifter – logic unit that can shift a data word any number of places in one clock cycle.

Baud – symbol rate; may or may not be the same as bit rate.

BCD – binary coded decimal. 4-bit entity used to represent 10 different decimal digits; with 6 spare states.

Big-endian – data format with the most significant bit or byte at the lowest address, or transmitted first.

Binary – using base 2 arithmetic for number representation.

BIOS – basic input output system; first software run after boot.

BIST – built-in self test.

Bit – smallest unit of digital information; two states.

Blackbox – functional device with inputs and outputs, but no detail on the internal workings.

Boolean – a data type with two values; an operation on these data types; named after George Boole, mid-19th century inventor of Boolean algebra.

Bootstrap – a startup or reset process that proceeds without external intervention.

Buffer – a temporary holding location for data.

Bug – an error in a program or device.

Bus – data channel, communication pathway for data transfer.

Byte – ordered collection of 8 bits; values from 0-255

C – programming language from Bell Labs, circa 1972.

Cache – faster and smaller intermediate memory between the processor and main memory.

Cache coherency – process to keep the contents of multiple caches consistent,

CAS – column address strobe (in DRAM refreshing)

Chip – integrated circuit component.

Clock – periodic timing signal to control and synchronize operations.

CMOS – complementary metal oxide semiconductor; a technology using both positive and negative semiconductors to achieve low power operation.

Complement – in binary logic, the opposite state.

Compilation – software process to translate source code to assembly or machine code (or error codes).

Control Flow – computer architecture involving directed flow through the program; data dependent paths are allowed.

Coprocessor – another processor to supplement the operations of the main processor. Used for floating point, video, etc. Usually relies on the main processor for instruction fetch; and control.

Core – early non-volatile memory technology based on ferromagnetic toroid's.

Cots – commercial, off-the-shelf.

CPU – central processing unit.

CRC – cyclic redundancy code, an error-control mechanism.

Dataflow – computer architecture where a changing value forces recalculation of dependent values.

Datagram – message on a packet switched network; the delivery, arrival time, and order of arrival are not guaranteed.

D-cache – data cache

DDR – dual data rate (memory).

Deadlock – a situation in which two or more competing actions are each waiting for the other to finish, and thus neither ever does.

DCE – data communications equipment; interface to the network.

Denorm – in floating point representation, a non-zero number with a magnitude less than the smallest normal number.

Device driver – specific software to interface a peripheral to the operating system.

Digital – using discrete values for representation of states or numbers.

Dirty bit – used to signal that the contents of a cache have changed.

DMA - direct memory access (to/from memory, for I/O devices).

Double word – two words; if word = 8 bits, double word = 16 bits.

Dram – dynamic random access memory.

DTE – data terminal equipment; communicates with the DCE to get to the network.

DVI – digital visual interface (for video).

ECL – emitter coupled logic, a bipolar transistor logic that is fast and power hungry.

EIA – Electronics Industry Association.

Epitaxial – in semiconductors, have a crystalline overlayer with a well-defined orientation.

Eprom – erasable programmable read-only memory.

EEprom – electrically erasable read-only memory.

Ethernet – 1980's networking technology. IEEE 802.3.

Exception – interrupt due to internal events, such as overflow.

FET – field effect transistor.

Fetch/execute cycle – basic operating cycle of a computer; fetch the instruction, execute the instruction.

Firewire – serial communications protocol (IEEE-1394).

Firmware – code contained in a non-volatile memory.

Fixed point – computer numeric format with a fixed number of digits or bits, and a fixed radix point. Integers.

Flag – a binary indicator.

Flash memory – a type of non-volatile memory, similar to EEprom.

Flip-flop – a circuit with two stable states; ideal for binary.

Floating point – computer numeric format for real numbers; has significant digits and an exponent.

FPGA – field programmable gate array.

FPU – floating point unit, an ALU for floating point numbers.

Full duplex – communication in both directions simultaneously.

Gate – a circuit to implement a logic function; can have multiple inputs, but a single output.

Giga - 10^9 or 2^{30}

GPU – graphics processing unit. ALU for graphics data.

GUI – graphics user interface.

Half-duplex – communications in two directions, but not simultaneously.

Handshake – co-ordination mechanism.

Harvard architecture – memory storage scheme with separate instructions and data.

Hexadecimal – base 16 number representation.

Hexadecimal point – radix point that separates integer from fractional values of hexadecimal numbers.

I-cache – instruction cache

IDE – Integrated development environment for software.

IEEE – Institute of Electrical and Electronic Engineers. Professional organization and standards body.

IEEE-754 – standard for floating point representation and operations.

Infinity - the largest number that can be represented in the number system.

Integer – the natural numbers, zero, and the negatives of the natural numbers.

Interrupt – an asynchronous event to signal a need for attention (example: the phone rings).

Interrupt vector – entry in a table pointing to an interrupt service routine; indexed by interrupt number.

I/O – Input-output from the computer to external devices, or a user interface.

IP – intellectual property; also internet protocol.

ISA – instruction set architecture, the software description of the computer.

ISA-32 – 32 bit instruction set architecture

ISA-64 = 64-bit instruction set architecture

ISO – International Standards Organization.

ISR – interrupt service routine, a subroutine that handles a particular interrupt event.

JTAG – Joint Test Action Group; industry group that lead to IEEE 1149.1, Standard Test Access Port and Boundary-Scan Architecture.

Junction – in semiconductors, the boundary interface of the n-type and p-type material.

Kernel – main portion of the operating system. Interface between the applications and the hardware.

Kilo – a prefix for 10^3 or 2^{10}

LAN – local area network.

Latency – time delay.

List – a data structure.

Little-endian – data format with the least significant bit or byte at the highest address, or transmitted last.

Logic operation – generally, negate, AND, OR, XOR, and their inverses.

Loop-unrolling – optimization of a loop for speed at the cost of space.

LRU – least recently used; an algorithm for item replacement in a cache.

LSB – least significant bit or byte.

LUT – look up table.

Mac – multiply-and-accumulate, operation for digital signal

processing,

Machine language – native code for a particular computer hardware.

Mainframe – a computer you can't lift.

Mantissa – significant digits (as opposed to the exponent) of a floating point value.

Master-slave – control process with one element in charge. Master status may be exchanged among elements.

Math operation – generally, add, subtract, multiply, divide.

Mega - 10^6 or 2^{20}

Memory leak – when a program uses memory resources but does not return them, leading to a lack of available memory.

Memory scrubbing – detecting and correcting bit errors.

Mesh – a highly connected network.

MESI – modified, exclusive, shared, invalid state of a cache coherency protocol.

Metaprogramming – programs that produce or modify other programs.

Microcode – hardware level data structures to translate machine instructions into sequences of circuit level operations.

Microcontroller – microprocessor with included memory and/or I/O.

Microkernel – operating system which is not monolithic. So functions execute in user space.

Microprocessor – a monolithic cpu on a chip.

Microprogramming – modifying the microcode.

MIL-STD-1553 – military standard (US) for a serial communications bus for avionics.

MIMD – multiple instruction, multiple data

Minicomputer – smaller than a mainframe, larger than a pc.

Minix – Unix-like operating system; free and open source.

MIPS – millions of instructions per second; sometimes used as a measure of throughput.

MMU – memory management unit; translates virtual to physical addresses.

Modem – modulator/demodulator; digital communications interface for analog channels.

MPU – memory protection unit – like an MMU, but without address translation.

MRAM – Magnetorestrictive random access memory. Non-volatile memory approach using magnetic storage elements and integrated circuit fabrication techniques.

MSB – most significant bit or byte.

Multiplex – combining signals on a communication channel by sampling.

Mutex – a data structure and methodology for mutual exclusion.

Multicore – multiple processing cores on one substrate or chip; need not be identical.

NAN – not-a-number; invalid bit pattern.

NAND – negated (or inverse) AND function.

NASA – National Aeronautics and Space Administration.

NDA – non-disclosure agreement; legal agreement protecting IP.

Nibble – 4 bits, ½ byte.

NIST – National Institute of Standards and Technology (US), previously, National Bureau of Standards.

NMI – non-maskable interrupt; cannot be ignored by the software.

NOR – negated (or inverse) OR function

Normalized number – in the proper format for floating point representation.

Null modem – acting as two modems, wired back to back. Artifact of the RS-232 standard.

NUMA – non-uniform memory access for multiprocessors; local and global memory access protocol.

NVM – non-volatile memory.

Octal – base 8 number.

Off-the-shelf – commercially available; not custom.

Opcode – part of a machine language instruction that specifies the operation to be performed.

Open source – methodology for hardware or software development with free distribution and access.

Operating system – software that controls the allocation of resources in a computer.

OSI – Open systems interconnect model for networking, from ISO.

Overflow - the result of an arithmetic operation exceeds the capacity of the destination.

Packet – a small container; a block of data on a network.

Paging – memory management technique using fixed size memory blocks.

Paradigm – a pattern or model.

Paradigm shift – a change from one paradigm to another. Can be disruptive or evolutionary.

Parallel – multiple operations or communication proceeding simultaneously.

Parity – an error detecting mechanism involving an extra check bit in the word.

PC – personal computer, politically correct, program counter.

PCB – printed circuit board.

PCI – peripheral interconnect interface (bus).

PCMCIA - Personal Computer Memory Card International Association, small card for memory expansion.

PDA – personal digital assistant. Small, hand-held computer like the Palm Pilot.

Peta - 10^{15} or 2^{50}

Pinout – mapping of signals to I/O pins of a device.

Pipeline – operations in serial, assembly-line fashion.

Pixel – picture element; smallest addressable element on a display or a sensor.

Posix – portable operating system interface, IEEE standard.

PROM – programmable read-only memory.

Quad word – four words. If word = 16 bits, quad word is 64 bits.

Queue – first in, first out data buffer structure; hardware of software.

RAID – random array of inexpensive disks; using commodity disk drives to build large storage arrays.

Radix point – separates integer and fractional parts of a real number.

RAM – random access memory; any item can be access in the same time as any other.

RAS – Row address strobe, in dram refresh.

Register – temporary storage location for a data item.

Reset – signal and process that returns the hardware to a known, defined state.

RISC – reduced instruction set computer.

ROM – read only memory.

Router – networking component for packets.

Real-time – system that responds to events in a predictable, bounded time.

RS-232 – EIA telecommunications standard (1962), serial with handshake.

SAM – sequential access memory, like a magnetic tape.

SATA – serial ATA, a storage media interconnect.

Sandbox – an isolated and controlled environment to run untested or potentially malicious code.

SDRAM – synchronous dynamic random access memory.

Segmentation – dividing a network or memory into sections.

Self-modifying code – computer code that modifies itself as it run; hard to debug

Semiconductor – material with electrical characteristics between conductors and insulators; basis of current technology processor and memory devices.

Semaphore –signaling element among processes.

Serial – bit by bit.

Server – a computer running services on a network.

Shift – move one bit position to the left or right in a word.

Sign-magnitude – number representation with a specific sign bit.

Signed number – representation with a value and a numeric sign.

SIMD – single instruction, multiple data.

Simm – single in-line memory module.

SOC – system on chip

Software – set of instructions and data to tell a computer what to do.

SMP – symmetric multiprocessing.

Snoop – monitor packets in a network, or data in a cache

SRAM – static random access memory.

Stack – first in, last out data structure. Can be hardware or software.

Stack pointer – a reference pointer to the top of the stack.

State machine – model of sequential processes.

Superscalar – computer with instruction-level parallelism, by replication of resources.

Synchronous – using the same clock to coordinate operations.

System – a collection of interacting elements and relationships with a specific behavior.

Table – data structure. Can be multi-dimensional.

Tera - 10^{12} or 2^{40}

Test-and-set – coordination mechanism for multiple processes that allows reading to a location and writing it in a non-interruptible manner.

TCP/IP – transmission control protocol/internet protocol; layered set of protocols for networks.

Thread – smallest independent set of instructions managed by a multiprocessing operating system.

TLB – translation lookaside buffer – a cache of addresses.

Transceiver – receiver and transmitter in one box.

TRAP – exception or fault handling mechanism in a computer; an operating system component.

Triplicate – using three copies (of hardware, software, messaging, power supplies, etc.). for redundancy and error control.

Truncate – discard. Cutoff, make shorter.

TTL – transistor-transistor logic in digital integrated circuits. (1963)

UART – universal asynchronous receiver-transmitter. Parallel-to-serial; serial-to parallel device with handshaking.

UDP – User datagram protocol; part of the Internet Protocol.

USART – universal synchronous (or) asynchronous receiver/transmitter.

Underflow – the result of an arithmetic operation is smaller than the smallest representable number.

USB – universal serial bus.

Unsigned number – a number without a numeric sign.

Vector – single dimensional array of values.

VHDL- very high level description language; a language to describe integrated circuits and asic/ fpga's.

VIA – vertical conducting pathway through an insulating layer in a semiconductor.

Virtual memory – memory management technique using address translation.

Virtualization – creating a virtual resource from available physical resources.

Virus – malignant computer program.

VLIW – very long instruction word – mechanism for parallelism.

von Neumann – John, a computer pioneer and mathematician; realized that computer instructions are data.

Wiki – the Hawaiian word for "quick." Refers to a collaborative content website.

Word – a collection of bits of any size; does not have to be a power of two.

Write-back – cache organization where the data is not written to main memory until the cache location is needed for re-use.

Write-only – of no interest.

Write-through – all cache writes also go to memory.

X86 – Intel -16, -32, 64-bit ISA.

XOR – exclusive OR; either but not both

Selected Bibliography

Computer Architecture

Bell, C. Gordon and Newell, Allen, *Computer Structures: Readings and Examples,* McGraw-Hill Inc., January 1, 1971, ISBN- 0070043574.

Blaauw, Gerrit A. and Brooks, Frederick P. Jr. *Computer Architecture, Concepts and Evolution,* 2 volumes, 1997, Addison-Wesley, IBN 0-201-10557-8.

Boole, George *An Investigation of the Laws of Thought on which are Founded the Mathematical Theories of Logic and Probability,*1854. Reprinted 1958, Dover, ISBN 0-486-60028-9.

Bruess, R. J. *RISC - The Mips-R3000 Family: Architecture, System Components, Compilers, Tools, Applications* , John Wiley & Sons Inc.,1991, ISBN 3800941031.

Bryant, Randal E. and O'Hallaron, David R. Computer systems: A Programmer's Perspective, 2nd edition, Addison Wesley, Kindle e-book edition, ASIN: B004S81RXE.

Burks, Arthur; W. Goldstein, Herman H.; Von Neumann, John Preliminary Discussion of the Logical Design of an Electronic Computing Instrument, 1987, MIT Press, originally published in Papers of John Von Neumann on Computing and Computer Theory.

Carter, Nick Schaum's *Outline of Computer Architecture,* McGraw-Hill; 1st edition (December 26, 2001) ISBN-007136207X.

Chow, Paul *The MIPS-X RISC Microprocessor,* 1989, Springer; ISBN 0792390458.

Comer, Douglas E. *Essentials of Computer Architecture,*

Prentice Hall; US Ed edition (August 23, 2004) ISBN 0131491792.

Dandamudi, Sivarama P. *Guide to RISC Processors: for Programmers and Engineers* Springer, 2010, ISBN 144191935X, ASIN: B001E3P3T0.

Englander, Irv *The Architecture of Computer Hardware and Systems Software: An Information Technology Approach*, Wiley; 3 edition (January 20, 2003) ISBN-0471073253.

Evans, James S.; Eckhouse, Richard H. *Alpha Risc Architecture for Programmers*, Prentice Hall, 1998, ISBN-0130814385.

Everett, R. R. and Swain, F. E. *Project Whirlwind, Report R-127, Whirlwind I Computer,* Servomechanisms Laboratory, M.I.T., Sept 4, 1947.

Flores, Ivan *The Logic of Computer Arithmetic,* 1963, Prentice-Hall, ISBN 0135400392.

Flynn, Michael J. *Computer Architecture: Pipelined and Parallel Processor Design,* 1995, Jones & Bartlett Learning; 1st ed, ISBN-0867202041.

Furber, S. B. *VLSI Risc Architecture and Organization* CRC Press; 1st ed, 1989, ISBN 0824781511.

Gaffney, David *RISC: The Intel I960 Family from A to Z,* RTC Books, 1996, ISBN 0929392299

Godse, A. P. *Microcontrollers & RISC Architecture*, Technical Publications; 1st. edition, 2011, ISBN- 9350380390.

Goodman, James; Miller, Karen *A Programmer's View of Computer Architecture: With Assembly Language Examples from the MIPS RISC Architecture,* Oxford University Press,

Preliminary ed., 1993, ISBN 0030972191.

Harris, David and Harris, Sarah *Digital Design and Computer Architecture*, Morgan Kaufmann (March 2, 2007) ISBN 0123704979.

Heath, Steve *Microprocessor Architectures, Second Edition: RISC, CISC and DSP* Newnes; 2nd ed, 1995, ISBN 0750623039.

Hennessy, John L. and Patterson, David A. *Computer Architecture, Fifth Edition: A Quantitative Approach*, Morgan Kaufmann; (September 30, 2011) ISBN 012383872X.

Patterson, David A., Hennessy, John L. *Computer Organization and Design The Hardware/Software Interface, ARM Edition,* Morgan Kaufman, 2017, ISBN 978-0-12-801733-3.

Heudin, J. C.; Panetto, C. *RISC Architectures* Springer; 1992 edition, 1992, ISBN 0412453401.

Heuring, Vincent, and Jordan, Harry F. *Computer Systems Design and Architecture* (2nd Edition), Prentice Hall; 2 edition (December 6, 2003) ISBN 0130484407.

Holt, Wayne E. (editor) Beyond *RISC! : An Essential Guide to Hewlett Packard Precision Architecture* Software Research Northwest, Incorporated (1988) ISBN 0961881372.

Johnson, William M. *Superscalar Microprocessors Design*, Prentice Hall PTR; Facsimile edition (December 11, 1990) ISBN 0138756341.

Kane, Gerry, *PA-RISC 2.0 Architecture*, Hewlett-Packard Professional Books, Prentice Hall; 1 edition, 1995, ISBN 0131827340.

Katevenis, Manolis G. H. *Reduced Instruction Set Computer Architectures for VLSI* The MIT Press, 1985, ISBN 0262111039.

Kidder, Tracy *The Soul of a New Machine*, Back Bay Books (June 2000) ISBN 0316491977.

Kuhnel, Claus, *AVR RISC Microcontroller Handbook*, Newnes; 1st edition, 1998, ISBN- 0750699639.

Mann, Daniel *Programming the 29K RISC Family*, Prentice Hall,1993, ISBN 0130918938.

Mano, M. Morris *Computer System Architecture* (3rd Edition), Prentice Hall; 3rd edition (October 29, 1992) ISBN 0131755633.

McGeady, Steven "The i960CA SuperScalar Implementation of the 80960 Architecture", IEEE, 1990, pp. 232–240.

Milutinovic, Veljko Surviving the Design of a 200 MHz RISC Micro- Processor: Lessons Learned, IEEE Press (1997) ASIN: B003KE2XJ4.

Motorola, MC88100 *RISC Microprocessors User's Manual*, Prentice Hall Trade; 2nd ed, 1989, ISBN 013567090X.

Murdocca, Miles J. and Heuring, Vincent *Computer Architecture and Organization: An Integrated Approach*, Wiley (March 16, 2007) ISBN 0471733881.

Nisan, Noam and Schocken, Shimon, *The Elements of Computing Systems: Building a Modern Computer from First Principles*, 2005, MIT Press, ISBN 0262640686.

Null, Linda *The Essentials of Computer Organization And Architecture*, Jones & Bartlett Pub; 2 edition (February 15, 2006) ISBN 0763737690.

Page, Daniel, *A Practical Introduction to Computer Architecture*, 2009, Springer, ISBN 1848822553.

Patterson, David A and Hennessy, John L. *Computer Organization and Design: The Hardware/Software Interface*, Revised Fourth Edition, Morgan Kaufmann; Nov. 2011 ISBN 0123744938.

Ramachandran, Umakishore, and Leahy William D. Jr., *Computer Systems: An Integrated Approach to Architecture and Operating Systems*, 2010, Addison Wesley, ISBN 0321486137.

Reid, T. R. *The Chip: How Two Americans Invented the Microchip and Launched a Revolution*, Random House Trade Paperbacks; Revised edition (October 9, 2001) ISBN 0375758283.

Richards, R. K. *Arithmetic Operations in Digital Computers, 1955, Van Nostrand,* B00128Z00.

Schmid, Hermann *Decimal Computation*, 1974, Wiley, ISBN 0-471-76180-X.

Severance, Charles; Dowd, Kevin *High Performance Computing (RISC Architectures, Optimization & Benchmarks)* O'Reilly Media; 2nd ed, 1998, ISBN 156592312X.

Shriver, Bruce D. *The Anatomy of a High-Performance Microprocessor: A Systems Perspective*, Wiley-IEEE Computer Society Press (June 4, 1998) ISBN 0818684003.

Sikha, Ed; Simpson, Rick; May, Cathy; Warren, Hank; *The PowerPC Architecture: A Specification for a New Family of RISC Processors* Morgan Kaufmann Pub; 2nd ed, 1994, ISBN 1558603166.

Silc, Jurji, Robic, Borut, Ungerer, Theo *Processor Architecture: From Dataflow to Superscalar and Beyond*, Springer; 1 edition (July 20, 1999) ISBN 3540647988.

Slater, Michael *A Guide to RISC Microprocessors*, Academic Press; 2nd ed. July 1992, ISBN-0126491402.

Slater, Michael Understanding RISC Microprocessors: 151 Articles Originally Published in Microprocessor Report Between March 1988 and April 1993, MICROPROCESSORS REPORT, Ziff Davis Press, 1993, ISBN 1562761595.

Somogyi, T Stephen *The PowerPC Macintosh: The Inside Story on the New RISC-Based Macintosh*   Addison-Wesley 1st ed, 1994, ISBN 0201626500.

Stallings, William *Computer Organization and Architecture: Designing for Performance* (7th Edition), Prentice Hall; 7 edition (July 21, 2005) ISBN 0131856448.

Stokes, Jon, *Inside the Machine An Illustrated Introduction to Microprocessors and Computer Architecture*, 2006, No Starch Press, ISBN 1593271042.

Sweetman, Dominic   *See MIPS Run,* Morgan Kaufmann; 2nd ed, 2006, ISBN 0120884216.

Tabak, Daniel; Curiel, A.   *RISC Architecture (Industrial Control, Computers & Communications)*   Research Studies Press, 1987, ISBN 0863800475.

Van Someren, Alex and Atack, Carol, *ARM RISC Chip: A Programmer's Guide*, 1994 Addison Wesley, ISBN 0201624109.

VL86C010 32 bit RISC CPU and Peripherals User's Manual, VLSI Technologies, Inc., 1989, Prentice-Hall, ISBN 0-13-

944968-X.

Waldron, John   *Introduction to RISC Assembly Language Programming*   Addison-Wesley; 1st edition, 1998, ISBN 0201398281.

Zengin, Salih *System-C Implementation of a RISC-Based Processor Architecture: Design and Implementation of a 16-bit RISC-based Processor Architecture with System-C Language,* VDM Verlag, March 22, 2009, ISBN- 3639130359.

Transputer

Inmos Digital Signal Processing Handbook, July 1989, Inmos Corp.

Transputer Databook, 2nd. edition, 1989, Inmos Corp.

Image Processing Databook, 1st. edition, Oct. 1990, SGS-Thompson Inmos.

The T9000 Transputer Products Overview Manual, 1991, SGS-Thompson Inmos.

Transputer Reference Manual, Inmos, Prentice Hall, 1988, ISBN 0-13-929001-X.

The Transputer Applications Notebook, Systems and Performance, 1989, Inmos Corp.

The Transputer Applications Notebook, Architecture and Software, 1989, Inmos Corp.

Roscoe & Hoare, *Laws Of Occam Programming*, 1986, Oxford University Computation Lab.

Theoharis, "Exploiting Parallelism In The Graphics Pipeline," 1985, Oxford University Computation Lab.Communicating Process Architecture, 1988, Prentice-Hall ISBN 0-13-629320-4

Turner "Some Issues In Scientific-Language Application Porting And Farming Using Transputers," Inmos Technical Note 53.

Poole "Example programs in the TDS," Inmos Technical Note 56.

Japp, "The Design Of A High Resolution Graphics System Using The IMS G300 Colour Video Controller," Inmos Technical Note 62.

The Transputer and The Toolset, Training Guide, Inmos.

The Military and Space Transputer Databook, 1990, Inmos.

McLean, Mick and Rowland, Tom *The Inmos Saga*, 1985, Frances Pinter (Publishers) Ltd. London, ISBN 0-86187-559-1.

Hinton, Jeremy and Alan Pinder; *Transputer Hardware And System Design*, 1993, Prentice Hall, TK7895.T73H56.

Mattos & Packer, "Using Transputers As Embedded Controllers," Inmos Technical Note 57.

Mattos, "The Transputer based Navigation System - An Example of Testing Embedded Systems," Inmos Technical Note 2.

"Under The Hood The Transputer Strikes Back. A Look At Inmos's Amazing New T9000 Transputer Chip," Aug 1991, Byte, v 16 n 8 p: 265.

Roberts, John; "Transputer Assembly Language Programming," 1992, Van Nostrand Reinhold.

Ellison, D.; "Understanding Occam And The Transputer : Through Complete, Working Programs," 1991, Sigma.

Mitchell, David A. P. "Inside the Transputer," 1990, Blackwell Scientific Publications.

SPARC

Cypress (Sparc) RISC Seminar notes, RISC 7C600, 1989.

"SPARC RISC User's Guide", Cypress Semiconductor, Feb. 1990, 2nd ed.

SPARC Architecture Manual (version 7) LSI Logic, 199x.

Bipolar Integrated Technology SPARC Overview, B5000, B5100, B5110/B5120, B5210.

"Superscalar Sparc chips offer performance gains, compatibility", Computer design July 1992 v 31 n 7 Page: 32.

Agrawal, A.; Garner, R. B.; "SPARC: A scalable processor architecture", Future Generations Computer Systems: FGCS, Apr 1992 v 7 n 2 / 3 Page: 303.

"Sparc Gets Smaller Still", Computer Design, Sept 1991 v 30 n 12 Page136.

MIPS

"MIPS RISC Architecture", Gerry Kane, Prentice Hall, 1988, ISBN 0-13-584293-X.

"System Design Using the MIPS R3000/3010 RISC Chipset", MIPS, IEEE Micro, 1989.

"A 10 mips 32 bit RISC Processor with 128 Mbytes/sec Bandwidth", Hudson et al, MIPS Computer Systems.

MIPS M/120 RISComputer Technical Overview, MIPS.

"The MIPS R3010 Floating Point Coprocessor", Rowen, Johnson, and Ries, IEEE Micro, June 1988.

LR3010/LR3010A MIPS Floating-Point Accelerator, User's

Manual, LSI Logic

LR3000/LR3000A Mips RISC Microprocessor User's Manual, LSI Logic.

LR33000 Self-Embedding Processor, User's Manual, LSI Logic.

IDT RISC, New Directions for MIPS RISC, 1990, IDT.

RISC Technology Seminar Workbook, 1989, 1990, IDT.

RISC Data Book, 1991, IDT.

RISC R3000 Family, Articles & Application Notes, IDT.

RISC R3000 Family Development Support Guide, 1991, IDT.

R3000/R3001 - Designers Guide, 1990, IDT.

IDT RISC R3001 RISController Handbook, IDT.

R3001 RISController Performance Comparison Report, IDT .

IDT, 1989 Data Book supplement, section 9 .

R3000 Family Hardware User's Manual, IDT.

Assembly Language Programmer's Guide, IDT.

System Programmer's Package Reference, IDT.

System Programmer's Guide, IDT.

"A High Performance Deterministic 79R3000-based Embedded System", Willenz, 9/89, IDT Applications note.
IDT7RS382 Theory of Operation, IDT.

R3051, Single-Chip RISC for Embedded Designs, IDT.

Vr3000, Advanced, High-Performance RISC Microprocessor, NEC Sept 89.

Vr3000 Series, RISC Microprocessor, Electrical Specifications, NEC.

Weiss, Ray; "Third-generation RISC processors", EDN, MAR 30 1992 v 37 n 7 Page: 96.

Cmelik, Robert F.; Ditzel, David R.; Kelly, Edmund J.; " An Analysis of SPARC and MIPS Instruction Set Utilization on the SPEC Benchmarks", Sigplan notices, APR 01 1991 v 26 n 4 Page: 290.

"RISC: the MIPS-R3000 family", published [by] Rolf-Jurgen Bruss. Berlin : Siemens Aktiengesellschaft, 1991

Vail, D. Estimating the On-Orbit Single Event Upset Behavior of a MIPS R3000 Microprocessor, Feb 1991, Harris Corporation.

IBM

Leaver, Mike; Sanghera, Hardev *IBM Risc System/6000 User Guide* McGraw-Hill,1993 ISBN 0077076877.

IBM *RISC System/6000 PowerPC System Architecture* Morgan Kaufmann; 1st ed. (September 15, 1994) ISBN 1558603441.

"IBM RISC System/6000 Technology", IBM Corp., 1990, SA23-2619.

Oehler, Richard R. ; Blasgen, Michael W.; "IBM RISC System/6000: Architecture and Performance", IEEE Micro, JUN 01 1991 v 11 n 3 Page: 14

Technical summary, PowerPC 601 RISC Microprocessor, Motorola, 4/93.

PowerPC 601 RISC Microprocessor User's Manual, 1993.

Motorola PowerPC 750 and PowerPC 740 Microprocessors, MPC750FACT/D, Rev. 4, Motorola.1999.

MPC740 RISC Microprocessor Technical summary, MPC750/D, 1997, Motorola.

RAD6000 Processor for Spaceborne Applications, June 1993, IBM Federal Systems.

iWarp

Figueiredo, Marco. "An Architectural Comparison between the Inmos Transputer T800 and the Intel iWARP Microprocessors," 1990, Loyola College, Dept. of Engineering Science.

iWarp Microprocessor, Intel, 1991, order 318153.

iWarp Programmers Guide, Intel, 318151.

iWarp Users Guide, Intel, 318158.

Introduction to iWARP, Intel, 318150.

References from Wikipedia

Flynn, Michael J. *Computer Architecture: Pipelined and Parallel Processor Design, 1995,* Jones & Bartlett Learning, 1st ed, ISBN 0867202041.

"Japanese 'K' Computer Is Ranked Most Powerful". The New York Times. 20 June 2011.

"Supercomputer "K computer" Takes First Place in World". Fujitsu. 2011.

Fisher, Joseph A.; Faraboschi, Paolo; Young, Cliff . *Embedded Computing: A VLIW Approach to Architecture, Compilers and*

Tools. 2005, ISBN 1558607668.

Milestones in Computer Science and Information Technology by Edwin D. Reilly 2003 ISBN 1-57356-521-0 .

Grishman, Ralph. Assembly Language Programming for the Control Data 6000 Series. Algorithmics Press. 1974.

Numerical Linear Algebra on High-Performance Computers by Jack J. Dongarra, et al 1987 ISBN 0-89871-428-1.

Processor Architecture: from Dataflow to Superscalar and Beyond by Jurij Šilc, Borut Robič, Theo Ungerer 1999 ISBN 3-540-64798-8.

Funding a Revolution: Government Support for Computing Research by Committee on Innovations in Computing and Communications, 1999, ISBN 0-309-06278-0

Processor Design: System-on-Chip Computing for ASICs and FPGAs by Jari Nurmi 2007 ISBN 1-4020-5529-3.

Readings in Computer Architecture by Mark Donald Hill, Norman Paul Jouppi, Gurindar Sohi 1999 ISBN 1-55860-539-8 .

-Patterson, David A.; Ditzel, David R. (1980). "The Case for the Reduced Instruction Set Computer". ACM SIGARCH Computer Architecture News 8 (6): 25–33. doi: 10.1145/641914.641917. CiteSeerX: 10.1.1.68.9623.

RISC I: A Reduced Instruction Set VLSI Computer by David A. Patterson and Carlo H. Sequin, in the Proceedings of the 8th annual symposium on Computer Architecture, 1981.

Design and Implementation of RISC I by Carlo Sequin and David Patterson, in the Proceedings of the Advanced Course on VLSI Architecture, University of Bristol, July 1982.

The MIPS-X RISC Microprocessor by Paul Chow 1989 ISBN 0-7923-9045-8.

Computer Science Handbook by Allen B. Tucker 2004 ISBN 1-58488-360-X.

"RISC vs. CISC: the Post-RISC Era" by Jon "Hannibal" Stokes (Ars Technica).

"RISC versus CISC" by Lloyd Borrett Australian Personal Computer, June 1991.

"Guide to RISC Processors for Programmers and Engineers": Chapter 3: "RISC Principles" by Sivarama P. Dandamudi, 2005, ISBN 978-0-387-21017-9.

"Microprocessors From the Programmer's Perspective" by Andrew Schulman 1990.

Kevin Dowd. High Performance Computing. O'Reilly & Associates, Inc. 1993.

"Schaum's Outline of Computer Architecture" by Nicholas P. Carter 2002 p. 96 ISBN 0-07-136207-X.

"CISC, RISC, and DSP Microprocessors" by Douglas L. Jones 2000.

"A History of Apple's Operating Systems" by Amit Singh.
Guide to RISC processors: for Programmers and Engineers by Sivarama P. Dandamudi - 2005 ISBN 0-387-21017-2.

If you enjoyed this book, you might also be interested in some of these.

Stakem, Patrick H. *16-bit Microprocessors, History and Architecture*, 2013 PRRB Publishing, ISBN-1520210922.

Stakem, Patrick H. *4- and 8-bit Microprocessors, Architecture and History*, 2013, PRRB Publishing, ISBN-152021572X,

Stakem, Patrick H. *Apollo's Computers,* 2014, PRRB Publishing, ISBN-1520215800.

Stakem, Patrick H. *The Architecture and Applications of the ARM Microprocessors,* 2013, PRRB Publishing, ISBN-1520215843.

Stakem, Patrick H. *Earth Rovers: for Exploration and Environmental Monitoring,* 2014, PRRB Publishing, ISBN-152021586X.

Stakem, Patrick H. *Embedded Computer Systems, Volume 1, Introduction and Architecture*, 2013, PRRB Publishing, ISBN-1520215959.

Stakem, Patrick H. *The History of Spacecraft Computers from the V-2 to the Space Station*, 2013, PRRB Publishing, ISBN-1520216181.

Stakem, Patrick H. *Floating Point Computation*, 2013, PRRB Publishing, ISBN-152021619X.

Stakem, Patrick H. *Architecture of Massively Parallel Microprocessor Systems*, 2011, PRRB Publishing, ISBN-1520250061.

Stakem, Patrick H. *Multicore Computer Architecture,* 2014, PRRB Publishing, ISBN-1520241372.

Stakem, Patrick H. *T. H. Paul & J. A. Millhollland: Master*

Locomotive Builders of Western Maryland, 2011, PRRB Publishing, ISBN-152019935X.

Stakem, Patrick H. *Personal Robots*, 2014, PRRB Publishing, ISBN-1520216254.

Stakem, Patrick H. *RISC Microprocessors, History and Overview*, 2013, PRRB Publishing, ISBN-1520216289.

Stakem, Patrick H. *Robots and Telerobots in Space Applications*, 2011, PRRB Publishing, ISBN-1520210361.

Stakem, Patrick H. *The Saturn Rocket and the Pegasus Missions, 1965*, 2013, PRRB Publishing, ISBN-1520209916.

Stakem, Patrick H. *Microprocessors in Space*, 2011, PRRB Publishing, ISBN-1520216343.

Stakem, Patrick H. Computer *Virtualization and the Cloud*, 2013, PRRB Publishing, ISBN-152021636X.

Stakem, Patrick H. *What's the Worst That Could Happen? Bad Assumptions, Ignorance, Failures and Screw-ups in Engineering Projects, 2014*, PRRB Publishing, ISBN-1520207166.

Stakem, Patrick H. *Computer Architecture & Programming of the Intel x86 Family, 2013*, PRRB Publishing, ISBN-1520263724.

Stakem, Patrick H. *The Hardware and Software Architecture of the Transputer*, 2011,PRRB Publishing, ISBN-152020681X.

Stakem, Patrick H. *Mainframes, Computing on Big Iron*, 2015, PRRB Publishing, ISBN- 1520216459.

Stakem, Patrick H. *Spacecraft Control Centers*, 2015, PRRB Publishing, ISBN-1520200617.

Stakem, Patrick H. *Embedded in Space,* 2015, PRRB Publishing,

ISBN-1520215916.

Stakem, Patrick H. *A Practitioner's Guide to RISC Microprocessor Architecture*, Wiley-Interscience, 1996, ISBN 0471130184.

Stakem, Patrick H. *Cubesat Engineeering*, PRRB Publishing, 2017, ISBN-1520754019.

Stakem, Patrick H. *Cubesat Operations*, PRRB Publishing, 2017, ISBN-152076717X.

Stakem, Patrick H. *Interplanetary Cubesats*, PRRB Publishing, 2017, ISBN-1520766173 .

Stakem, Patrick H. Cubesat Constellations, Clusters, and Swarms, Stakem, PRRB Publishing, 2017, ISBN-1520767544.

Stakem, Patrick H. *Graphics Processing Units, an overview*, 2017, PRRB Publishing, ISBN-1520879695.

Stakem, Patrick H. *Intel Embedded and the Arduino-101, 2017,* PRRB Publishing, ISBN-1520879296.

Stakem, Patrick H. *Orbital Debris, the problem and the mitigation*, 2018, PRRB Publishing, ISBN-*1980466483*.

Stakem, Patrick H. *Manufacturing in Space*, 2018, PRRB Publishing, ISBN-1977076041.

Stakem, Patrick H. , *NASA's Ships and Planes*, 2018, PRRB Publishing, ISBN-1977076823.

Stakem, Patrick H. *Space Tourism*, 2018, PRRB Publishing, ISBN-1977073506.

Stakem, Patrick H. *STEM – Data Storage and Communications*, 2018, PRRB Publishing, ISBN-1977073115.

Stakem, Patrick H. *In-Space Robotic Repair and Servicing*, 2018, PRRB Publishing, ISBN-1980478236.

Stakem, Patrick H. *Introducing Weather in the pre-K to 12 Curricula, A Resource Guide for Educators*, 2017, PRRB Publishing, ISBN-1980638241.

Stakem, Patrick H. *Introducing Astronomy in the pre-K to 12 Curricula, A Resource Guide for Educators*, 2017, PRRB Publishing, ISBN-198104065X.
Also available in a Brazilian Portuguese edition, ISBN-1983106127.

Stakem, Patrick H. *Deep Space Gateways, the Moon and Beyond*, 2017, PRRB Publishing, ISBN-1973465701.

Stakem, Patrick H. *Crewed Spacecraft*, 2017, PRRB Publishing, ISBN-1549992406.

Stakem, Patrick H. *Rocketplanes to Spacecraft*, 2017, PRRB Publishing, ISBN-1549992589.

Stakem, Patrick H. *Crewed Space Stations,* 2017, PRRB Publishing, ISBN-1549992228.

Stakem, Patrick H. *,Enviro-bots for STEM: Using Robotics in the pre-K to 12 Curricula, A Resource Guide for Educators,* 2017, PRRB Publishing, ISBN-1549656619.

Stakem, Patrick H. *STEM-Sat, Using Cubesats in the pre-K to 12 Curricula, A Resource Guide for Educators*, 2017, ISBN-1549656376.

Stakem, Patrick H. *Visiting the NASA Centers, and Locations of Historic Rockets and Spacecraft,* 2107, PRRB Publishing, ISBN-154965120X.

Stakem, Patrick H. *Lunar Orbital Platform-Gateway*, 2018, PRRB Publishing, ISBN-1980498628.

Stakem, Patrick H. Embedded GPU's, 2018, PRRB Publishing, ISBN- 1980476497.

Stakem, Patrick H. Mobile Cloud Robotics, 2018, PRRB Publishing, ISBN- 1980488088

Stakem, Patrick H. *Extreme Environment Embedded Systems* 2017, PRRB Publishing, ISBN-1520215967.

Stakem, Patrick H. *What's the Worst, Volume-2*, 2018, ISBN-1981005579.

Stakem, Patrick H., *Spaceports*, 2018, ISBN-1981022287.

Stakem, Patrick H., *Space Launch Vehicles*, 2018, ISBN-1983071773.

Stakem, Patrick H. *Mars*, 2018, ISBN-1983116902.

Stakem, Patrick H. *X-86, 40th Anniversary ed*, 2018, ISBN-1983189405.

Stakem, Patrick H. *Intel Embedded and the Arduino-101, 2017,* PRRB Publishing, ISBN-1520879296.

Stakem, Patrick H. *Lunar Orbital Platform-Gateway*, 2018, PRRB Publishing, ISBN-1980498628.

Stakem, Patrick H. *Space Weather*, 2018, ISBN-1   723904023.

Stakem, Patrick H. *STEM-Engineering Process*, 2017,   ISBN-1983196517.

2018 Releases

Space Telescopes

Exoplanets

www.ingramcontent.com/pod-product-compliance
Lightning Source LLC
Chambersburg PA
CBHW031246050326
40690CB00007B/970